MARMOSETS IN MASTRICK

A Brief History of Aberdeen Zoo

Robert J Leslie

This publication should be cited as:

Marmosets in Mastrick – A Brief History of Aberdeen Zoo

Cover design, printing and binding by RGU Gatehouse, Aberdeen (2020)

ISBN 978-1-9999882-2-7

Contents

About the Author

Rob Leslie was born and brought up in Aberdeen. He was educated at
Summerhill Secondary School and Aberdeen Grammar.

Although the natural world had a big influence on his formative years, a career in
construction beckoned. He was a chartered construction manager, a chartered quantity
surveyor and was appointed as Honorary Professor at Robert Gordon University.
In the six years before he retired, he was full-time lecturer and subject leader at
Scott Sutherland School, Robert Gordon University.

Nature and the environment have played an important part throughout his life and his
involvement with the Young Ornithologists Club in the late 80s and 90s reinforced his
love of birds. This not only helped keep his sanity but endowed him with life-long
friends and an interest which he is passing onto his grandchildren.

He continues to live in Aberdeen with his wife, Irene.
He has two sons, David and Peter.

I would like to dedicate this book to my family, especially my grandchildren Ruaridh, Murray and Amy.....and of course Zoey who will never get to hear Grandpa's tales of the Zoo.

Acknowledgements

I am firstly indebted to my father, George Leslie, who kept the minutes of meetings, press cuttings and photographs which allowed me to complete this book. I have also included a section that my father had written, presumably with the intent of writing a book which he never completed.

My father was my hero for the first decade of my life. He had been brought up at Viewbank, the family market garden business and this upbringing had endowed him with a great physical strength. His party trick was seemingly to bend old penny pieces between the fingers of one hand. It was rather ironic that one so physically strong had a weakness when it came to alcohol. My father started drinking when my grandmother died. I think she had been incredibly strict with him regarding drink, because his father had been an alcoholic. I remember a play on TV many years ago. In discussing one of the characters, they said drink didn't choose him, he chose drink, and so it was with my father. I wanted to state this now to get it out in the open as a lot of the people involved with the Zoo would have thought it a serious omission otherwise. I think it's appropriate to acknowledge that my mother and I lived through some unpredictable and interesting times. It is all credit to my mother that she supported my father, not only as a dutiful wife, but also as his secretary for the Zoo and in his roles as President of Aberdeen Aquarist Society, Vice President of Aberdeen Cat Club, Secretary and Treasurer of WWF and Chairman of 14th Boy Scouts Parents Committee. She was also veterinary nurse to a wide variety of creatures which had to be cared for in the house, manager of the Zoo shop, organiser of the staff rotas and all the while making excuses when my father was 'unwell'. I think it is fair to say that my mother does not look back on the days of the Zoo with fond memories, but that was more due to my father's drinking than the workload, the staff or the animals.

Despite my father's drinking, there is no questioning his devotion and commitment to the Zoo and the animals in his care; a fact commented on many times through the course of the years. He and my mother received many acknowledgements in minutes of meetings and correspondence regarding their dedication and, even when my father was asked to resign, there are expressions of the important part that they played in the life of the Zoo. Prof. Eric Salzen, the last Convenor of the Aberdeen and North of Scotland Zoological Society, acknowledged my parents' contribution at the demise of the Zoo saying '*His care of the animals was exceedingly good and the amount of effort he and his wife put in was tremendous*'.

When my father died, I was incredibly grateful for the things he had taught me and the values which he espoused, but at the same time I was sorry for the things that might have been during the Zoo years and beyond.

Thanks are also due to my long-suffering wife, Irene, who has listened to me talk about this book for many years, my sons, David and Peter, for encouraging me to put pen to paper and my family and many friends who listened as I no doubt bored them witless with tales of my life as an inmate of Aberdeen Zoo.

I would also like to acknowledge the contributions from the following: D.C. Thomson & Co Ltd. for newspaper articles, University of Aberdeen - Special Collections Centre for the architect's drawings and minutes of meetings, and Gordon Ferrier, Witek Mojsiewicz and Scotsman Publications for the photographs. My sincere thanks to Mark and Fran Sullivan for their patience, persistence and dedication in editing, formatting, grammar and spelling correction as without them this book may still have been a pile of notes and newspaper cuttings.

Any errors are mine and mine alone. I have utilised the information contained in the minutes of meetings, press articles and notes to produce this book in good faith.

Robert J Leslie (October 2020)

Dad and Kestrel

Introduction

After a few false starts I have eventually managed to put pen to paper and record the events which resulted in the establishment of Aberdeen Zoo in the 1960s. I would not have started this book if it had not been for my good friend and birdwatching mentor Mark Sullivan. It all started with me regaling Mark with stories of my teenage years and my involvement with the early years of the Zoo. This started out as a series of anecdotes, some funny, others a bit more serious, but it was soon apparent that I needed to expand the original scope to add details of how the Zoo came into existence and to recognise the hard work and contribution made by so many.

Over the course of the next few chapters I will try and give a potted history of the Zoo along with my recollection of events. These are before the Zoo was a physical reality and after my father, mother and I moved into the Manager's House in 1967. This explains how a young lad from Mastrick ended up with Aberdeen Zoo as his address.

There were many laughs and tears along the way. Many of the keepers were deeply attached to the animals in their care and, as many of you who have pets will know, when they die it fills you with all the sense of bereavement that losing a loved one brings.

As I recall the various episodes from the early 1960s to the mid-1970s, I am sure I will have forgotten to mention many who played an important role in the formation of the Zoo and to them I apologise. I have had to rely on notes which my father left, minutes of management and committee meetings, press cuttings and the contents of three archive boxes held by the University of Aberdeen - Special Collections Centre in the Sir Ian Duncan Rice Library. These are augmented by my recollection of events as my main sources for this book. In addition, I have included eight 'chapters' in Part Three of the book which were written by my father as part of a book which he never finished. I think it is only right that I include his work as this reflects the dedication he exhibited in ensuring the wellbeing of the animals in his charge both prior to and after the opening of the Zoo.

One of the fundamental questions in all this is which comes first: the zoo or the animals? If you build a zoo but have no animals no one will come, if you have animals what do you do with them while the zoo is being built?

Another question to be answered is how an assistant post-mortem attendant and hospital porter at Aberdeen Royal Infirmary became involved with setting up the

Zoo in Aberdeen, eventually becoming manager.

Prior to my father's involvement with the Aberdeen and North of Scotland Zoological Society, to give its proper title, we had always kept pets. My father had been brought up on the family's market garden and smallholding at Viewbank, Aberdeen. Viewbank was located approximately where Cairncry Road sits today. The land was purchased by Aberdeen City Council to construct much needed council housing.

When the market garden closed, my father became a hospital porter at Aberdeen Royal Infirmary. He was not an 'educated' man by the standards of the time, but he was an intelligent man who read books on a wide variety of topics, many of them on the natural world, and retained a huge knowledge of many subjects. From the beginnings as a hospital porter he became an assistant post-mortem attendant, a rather gruesome sounding role, but one which taught him about the workings of the body. These lessons in human physiology were useful and transferable. When animals died, he was able to carry out post-mortems to establish the cause of death.

When my father and mother married, they shared a house with my grandmother at Smithfield Drive. I was born into this household and I always remember animals being part of my life. Smithfield Drive was home to rabbits, guinea pigs, hens, snakes and a dog, Judy. My mother always says that Judy would stay by my pram and make sure I did not come to any harm. It was generally a more trusting time when prams were left out for infants to get fresh air. I don't know if the threat of anything happening to you has increased over the years, but it is disappointing when I hear of children being restricted because of the fear brought on by media coverage.

When I was about five years old my parents were allocated a council house of their own and we moved to Sheddocksley Road in Mastrick. I cannot remember animals being transported from Smithfield to Mastrick, but it was not long before they were housed in the shed and hutches in the back garden and cages within the house. In addition to the run-of-the-mill rabbits, guinea pigs and hamsters we kept a farmyard duck, owls, slow worms and a large tropical spider. Rabbits and guinea pigs were housed in the back garden. I recall that we decided to have a couple of hamsters. However, once my father realised that they were easy to breed with a market in selling the offspring to the local pet shops, the shed was given over to 'Leslie's Hamster Stud Farm'.

The farmyard duck was by far and away the main character of the collection. Blackie was part of a small flock of ducks that wandered about the farmyard at a relative's farm beside Huntly. Blackie could not keep up with the rest of the flock because of

Me and Blackie in the back garden at Mastrick

a damaged leg and I took pity on the bird. We took it back to Aberdeen and Blackie was kept in the back garden. He became very tame and would chase you across the garden and would accompany you when there was any digging to be done; he would hoover up the exposed cache of worms. Many younger readers will not realise that we lived in a simpler time and it was quite the thing to have Pet Shows. All the kids used to take along their rabbits, guinea pigs, cats and a variety of mongrels. A duck was an unusual entrant at these events, but Blackie was very friendly and a hit with most who attended. Blackie and I also starred in the Grampian TV's children's show 'Romper Room'.

Now I know that we as a race think that animals do not have emotions, but one foggy night we heard a duck flying overhead and it landed in the garden. We took the duck in and fed and watered it. The next day Blackie was dead, sitting bolt upright in his hutch. We never did find out why he died.

All of this animal husbandry, along with his interest in the natural world, a prodigious amount of reading and an excellent memory, equipped my father with an exceptional knowledge of animals and their care. Like many others of my father's generation, the natural world was a source of food and I was taught to shoot and fish, but it was always for the pot. The hunting of animals also provided my father with an understanding of the animals' natural habitat and food, which in a way became part of the source of animal husbandry. It therefore seemed quite natural that when my father saw the notification of the inaugural meeting of the Aberdeen and North of Scotland Zoological Society he would go along. This initial interest soon developed into a substantial part of our lives as my father farmed out animals which were donated prior to the Zoo being built, along with taking a travelling menagerie round to various Highland Games to raise funds for the building of the Zoo. He also used the commercial skills learned at the market garden to reduce the potential food bills.

The Zoo was the idea of Dr Lil de Kock of the University of Aberdeen's Zoology Department who, with like-minded individuals back in the early 1960s, was determined to make a zoo in Aberdeen a reality. As you will see it took perseverance on behalf of these founding fathers to bring it to fruition. It is also worth noting that from the inaugural meeting at Aberdeen Town House on 28th September 1961, the Zoo was built, stocked and officially opened within four and half years.

The discussions centred around the formation of a small zoo (around 12 acres in area) concentrating on indigenous Scottish animals, past and present.

The discussions went so far as to propose two sites, one at Hazlehead and one at Denwood.

Although there was no conclusion at the meeting, it is obvious that there was an appetite to progress the plans to make Aberdeen Zoo a reality.

A Foundation Meeting was held on 6th December 1961 at which a development plan was tabled. The proposal was to establish a small zoo in an area to the east of Hazlehead Restaurant with a subsequent development of up to 20 acres at Denwood. The emphasis on the collection was to be of native Scottish animals.

The initial plans were shared with the public at a meeting in April 1962.

As a result of the formation of the Aberdeen and North of Scotland Zoological Society the house at Mastrick started to see some more exotic residents. A rustic aviary was attached to the rear wall of the property and over the years it housed owls, pheasants, a capercaillie and some quail.

Visitors to the house could not help but notice the tall cage in the living room which housed our cotton-eared marmosets. Initially we had one male cotton-eared marmoset, Sinni, which was bought from a livestock dealer in England and subsequently donated to the Zoo. Had the story ended there, the title of this book would have been 'Marmoset in Mastrick'. However, this is where fate took a hand.

About four months after Sinni's arrival we noticed that between 8.30 and 9.30 am he sat looking out of our south-facing window and started emitting a very high-pitched whistle. The whistle, at times, could not be heard in the same room, but was audible upstairs or in the adjoining rooms. It transpired that, by chance, a family who stayed about three quarters of a mile from us also had a marmoset, a female. This female slept indoors at night and was allowed free run of the greenhouse during the day. We later found out that at the same time as Sinni was whistling and looking to the south, the female was looking towards our house and whistling. The female

Mum feeding the Marmoset at home

was named Chico and had been bartered for a packet of 20 cigarettes in Rio de Janeiro and was brought back to the UK in the spring of 1963. By chance the family came to stay in the new suburb of Mastrick. On hearing about our male marmoset and the plans for the Zoo, they donated the female to the Zoo.

The two marmosets had different characters; Sinni was more reserved, but Chico was an extrovert and completely unafraid. When one of our Siamese cats sat on top of the marmosets' cage to enjoy the warmth from the heat lamp, Chico would try and push the cat off, even going as far as pulling its tail. Sinni and Chico went on to produce twins every year from 1963 to 1967, hence the book is quite rightly entitled 'Marmosets in Mastrick'.

Marmosets are easily kept in captivity and fed on a diet of fruit and mealworms. The living room was also home to a couple of aquaria of tropical fish. In my bedroom was a tank containing stick insects. Whilst my father was a porter at the hospital one of his duties was to drive the manageress of the hospital shops, Miss Smart, to Veitch Moir to purchase fruit. On one of these buying trips a large spider was found in the bananas. We were told it was a huntsman spider. Boris, as he became known, was saved by my father and taken home where he was kept in an old battery jar in

Sinni and Chico with their five-week old twins

the cupboard in my bedroom which housed the hot water tank. Boris was fed on live flies. Boris moved with astonishing speed; you were aware of a movement and then he was back in his original position, but holding a fly in his jaws.

All these animals made for interesting conversations when visitors came to the house, but unfortunately it made us a target for the local yobs. One night we came home to find graffiti on the front wall of the house, and I remember my mother being very upset. Thankfully, this was an isolated incident.

Although the house was home to many animals, I do not recall any complaints from the neighbours as we

Me in my bedroom at Mastrick

did not have animals that were too big, too noisy or too smelly to upset the local families. They probably just thought we were just a bit odd.

As I reflect on the early days of the Zoo, I cannot help but question the place in our modern world for zoos, but back in the 1950s and 60s they were more acceptable. Without zoos many people would never have seen an elephant or a lion. Back then, as the UK emerged from post-war austerity, who would have predicted that foreign travel would have been available to the average man in the street. There is also an argument that well-run zoos, where the animals' welfare, not the number of visitors is the priority, have contributed to saving many species from extinction.

Our relationship with the natural world has changed so much over the last 100 years. I recently read 'Water for Elephants', by Sara Gruen, which is set in America in the early 1990s and is about travelling circus shows. Although it is a work of fiction it demonstrates that the public had to rely on these travelling menageries to see exotic animals which they had only seen in magazines and encyclopaedias. The animal husbandry left a lot to be desired. Roll forward to when the Zoo was opened in the 1960s, and you have Sir David Attenborough embarking on his Zoo Quest series to exotic parts of the world. He was being funded not only to film these animals in the wild, but also to capture specimens for London Zoo.

These were indeed different times and I would now be more comfortable with George Monbiot's vision of rewilding the British countryside rather than consigning animals and birds to a life of captivity. However, I realise that zoos do play a vital part in saving species from extinction.

Growing up in the 1960s we had more freedom to explore the natural world; there were not the electronic and technological distractions which are around today. It also felt a safer time; my friends and I were out most of the day playing in the local woods and our parents were more relaxed about it.

It is rather ironic that we are now recognising the benefits of the natural world on our mental health. In Shetland doctors are even prescribing exposure to the natural world to alleviate the symptoms of depression.

We are seeing the degradation of the natural world as greater areas of forest are being felled to make way for cash crops. We cannot blame the indigenous people for their actions; after all they just want a better lifestyle more akin to us in the developed world. Meanwhile we are trying to reconnect with the natural world.

It should be incumbent on all of mankind to use the finite earth's resources carefully as we cannot continue to exploit the natural world when we know that on our present consumption levels, we in the UK would need about three planets worth of resources to satisfy our demands to the detriment of our children and grandchildren.

Part One – History of the Zoo

The Early Years

I t will surprise many to know the Zoo at Hazlehead was not the first zoo in Aberdeen. The first 'zoo' was in the unlikely setting of the Alhambra Music Hall, at the corner of Guild Street and Exchange Street. This small zoo was opened by John Sinclair in 1906.

The small zoo was reported as showing *'this fine zoological collection…which has largely been augmented by African and Nubian lions, black and brown bears, wolves, hyenas, antelopes, gazelles, llamas etc., and a host of foreign birds, monkeys and reptiles from all quarters of the globe'.*

What happened to the animals is not recorded, but sometime later the premises are recorded as home to offices.

From here 'the Zoo' refers to Aberdeen Zoo at Hazlehead, and 'the Society' refers to the Aberdeen and North of Scotland Zoological Society including all the various committees. Any mention of Aberdeen City Council refers to Aberdeen City

Dr Lil de Kock with Foxie (left) and Honey Badger (right)

Council in all its various iterations i.e. Aberdeen Town Council, Aberdeen District Council etc.

How do you start a zoo when all you have is the basic idea, bags of enthusiasm and not much else?

Dr Lil de Kock spearheaded the 'Zoo Project', as it was entitled, with a group of academics from the University of Aberdeen with the full support of Professor V.C. Wynne-Edwards.

Lil could be described as the driving force behind the Aberdeen Zoo Project. She had a colourful background; she was courageous in her opposition to Hitler in her homeland of Germany, eventually being imprisoned for helping British soldiers to escape. Lil herself managed to escape and made it to Britain in a rowing boat across the English Channel. She had been forbidden to study Zoology in Germany, but she was able to study in Britain eventually becoming a lecturer at Aberdeen University.

Lilias Gourdie, a journalist at Aberdeen Journals, who was a great supporter and author of many of the press articles about the Zoo, noted in June 1968 *'I've read too about her long and persistent fight to persuade Aberdeen Town Council to provide facilities for a zoo in the city. And had often wondered how one woman, in the face of so many setbacks and opposition in life, could have done so much..... Meeting her, I could understand how this one woman had bullied, cajoled and wheedled her way to seeing the foundation of her pet project, the zoo.'*

Lil and others from the Zoology Department at the University must have had various informal meetings to gather their thoughts and establish a plan of action, but there is no record of these and we can only surmise the discussions as they, possibly with a little naivety, approached Aberdeen City Council.

On 28th September 1961 a Private and Confidential Informal Meeting was held at the Town House. I think it is important to record the attendees at this meeting as they effectively gave birth to the idea of Aberdeen Zoo.

Lord Provost Graham, Dr Lil de Kock, Mr Rennie (Town Clerk), Professor V.C. Wynne-Edwards, Professor T.C. Phemister, Dr A.T. Phillipson (Rowett), Dr D.T. Gauld, Dr J.D. Nisbet, Mr Winning (Links and Parks), Mr Collie, Mr Keith (City Architect) and Campbell Connon (Solicitor).

The list of attendees and their respective seniority in their organisations demonstrates the seriousness of the venture.

At the meeting it was agreed to progress with the plans to provide a small zoo of 12 acres. The area of the land allocated to the Zoo Project is significant and will prove to be extremely important and contentious in the years ahead.

The Zoo was to be a 'Geographical Zoo concentrating on indigenous Scottish animals'.

It was planned to provide housing for the animals but without heating to keep the costs down.

The proposed sites were discussed, with Hazlehead and Denwood being recorded in the minutes.

Under the heading of Finance, it was suggested that approximately £15,000 was deemed necessary to create the necessary Keeper's house, small animal hospital, (it doesn't clarify if this was a hospital for small animals or whether it was a small building) and also the provision of the necessary enclosures.

Having been in the construction industry for 47 years, I cannot understand how a budget could be determined at such an early stage with no drawings, details or even an agreed site.

By way of showing the commercial viability of zoos, examples were given of Dudley Zoo which was a profitable private venture and Edinburgh Zoo which was a private venture with any deficit being underwritten by Edinburgh City Council.

From this initial meeting a Foundation Meeting was held on 6th December 1961, where the development plans included a small area adjacent to Hazlehead Restaurant with a subsequent development of up to 20 acres of Denwood. The emphasis was still to be on natural Scottish animals.

During these early days it was deemed that no formal affiliation with the Royal Scottish Zoological Society was desirable. Looking back, it is interesting to speculate if this decision was misplaced, as in 1977 when the Zoo was in trouble, Roger Wheater from the Royal Scottish Zoological Society, based in Edinburgh, made an appeal to Aberdeen City Council to save the Zoo.

Once the proposals were made public, the reaction was positive. The local press supported the idea and interviews were carried out on radio and Grampian Television.

As we will see, education was the core aim of the Society and an informal meeting of head teachers and principal teachers of science from all the city schools was held on 19th February 1962 at which 75 teachers attended.

Engagement with the general public started with a meeting in the YMCA on 27th

February 1962 with between 70 and 80 people attending to hear about the proposals for a zoo in Aberdeen.

But how do you keep everyone enthused about the scheme when there was no agreed site? Suggestions were made for a little zoo to begin with, or even a mobile zoo to visit the schools which would showcase the animals to children. Details of the 'Little Zoo' included a mouse town, a beehive, an aquarium or vivarium, an aviary, a monkey island, an insect house, a children's corner, chicken hutches, a reptile house, a mole colony and Scottish Alpine plants.

One town councillor thought that the buildings appeared whimsical, as you will see from the initial images of the proposed buildings.

The support from Aberdeen City Council continued and Mr Winning gave a guided tour of the proposed site at Hazlehead in May 1962. I seem to recollect at this time that Mr Winning could foresee Hazlehead Park and surrounding area being a weekend oasis for the family. I remember clearly a set of sketches which showed the bridging over the road, utilising a pedestrian bridge similar to those used for railway lines, to allow expansion into the land currently occupied by the pitch and putt/Footgolf and rugby pitches. As mentioned in the introduction, there was a different attitude then, but Mr Winning could foresee a time when dad would play golf at Hazlehead, while mum took the kids to the Zoo, which would eventually occupy the whole of Hazlehead Park whilst retaining the specimen trees. As we will see the dreams and aspirations were not to be fulfilled for various reasons.

In tandem with the development of the plans for the Zoo there was the need to fundraise.

Fundraising

It is sometimes difficult to differentiate publicity events from purely fundraising initiatives. It was to satisfy these dual outcomes that my father, mother and myself, along with many others, pitched our marquees and delivered the animals and enclosures to various shows around the North East of Scotland. In 1962 the travelling menagerie pitched up at the Banchory Show and the Aberdeen Highland Games. All was well when the weather was good, but if it rained it required the swift distribution of duck boards to save the grass areas becoming a quagmire.

One of the biggest events undertaken was a three-day Christmas Show which was held in the YMCA on Union Street, adjacent to the Music Hall. I should point out that this was not the building that we see today which houses a couple of mini supermarkets, charity shops and a betting shop on the ground floor, but the previous premises which you entered directly off Union Street. To accompany this public event a brochure was produced entitled 'A Zoo for You'.

The show was held from 26-28th December 1962 and it was reported that 1,472 adults and 1,469 children attended, along with 332 members who were entitled to free entry. In addition to the exhibits the crowds had to be catered for and refreshments had to be offered.

This formula was repeated in July 1963 with a Pets Corner at the Royal Northern Agricultural Show. At the end of August there was a three-day event at Aberdeen Highland Games. In September that year there was a two-day show of invertebrates in the Music Hall.

As you can imagine these shows, together with the more regular fundraising activities, not to mention the actual planning for the Zoo and the temporary housing of donated animals, required a huge effort and commitment from many volunteers. It is matter of regret that I cannot mention them all by name, but I am sure that many Aberdonians will remember their experiences back in the swinging sixties which had more to do with mucking out animals than sex and drugs and rock and roll!

The fundraising efforts of all the Society's committees were also widely covered, from the Badger's Ball held in Kirk House in Belmont Street where you could dance the night away to the music of the Misfits (I wonder what ever happened to them). I remember that event well, not for the dancing, but for an altercation at the entrance. I had broken my arm which was in a plaster cast. Some young lads decided they did not want to come in, but thought it would be a jolly wheeze to take the decorated hardboard cut-outs of animals with them. When they were stopped by me and others on the door, one decided to take a swing at me using the cut-outs. Imagine the lad's surprise when I defended myself with the plaster cast. He couldn't understand why I wasn't writhing in agony. But common sense on the part of his pals prevailed when they saw I was plastered, which may be applied to them as well, and they decided to leave.

In addition to these shows other activities were held such as Cheese and Wine Parties in April 1964.

As the Zoo became a physical reality, the need for funds became even more pressing and a dance was held in the Palace Ballroom in October 1966.

As well as these more unique events, more traditional fundraising activities were utilised to swell the coffers. Jumble sales were held in St Catherine's Club, Raffles and Bring and Buy Sales were to the fore, and woe betide any of my teachers or fellow pupils at Summerhill Secondary School if they didn't have a pencil - as quick as flash I would produce an Aberdeen Zoo branded pencil to sell to them. It is perhaps a sign of the times that in 1963 funds were raised through a Bridge Tournament. I doubt if there are many organisations that would see this as a fundraising opportunity today.

Once the Zoo was in operation there was the opportunity to sell commemorative items to be brought home as a memento from a trip to Aberdeen Zoo. All round the country there are probably charity shops which now have ceramic egg cups, playing card holders and tea strainers all branded with Aberdeen Zoo.

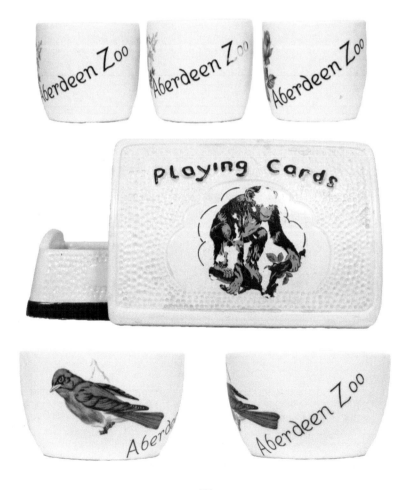

Funding the Zoo was always a bit of a struggle as there were only four sources of income: ticket sales, the sale of refreshments and merchandise, donations from members of the public and the sale of surplus animals. As we will see, the lack of funds was a contributory factor in the demise of the Zoo.

Farming out the Animals

There was also the obvious problem of animals - do you build a zoo and then acquire them, or do you acquire them and build a zoo? The problem became more of an issue when the plans went public and members of the public wanted to donate animals. There is even a record of an Aberdonian living in India offering his tame leopard to the Zoo; finding a temporary home for that may have been a challenge!

One of the organisations which was most supportive in the early years was Oakbank School, an approved school for young boys with behavioural difficulties. The staff and boys looked after a few of the animals in one of their outhouses. This arrangement benefitted both the boys and the Zoo. It gave the boys something to do as they served their time and all the Zoo had to do was supply the material for cages and the food for the animals.

The arrangement was working well until the incident with the Colonel. The Colonel was a male Mona monkey with a beautiful face and incisors the size of a man's little finger. One of the boys insisted on tormenting the Colonel at every opportunity, poking sticks into the cage and generally annoying the poor beast. One day, one of the other boys thought it would be good to let the Colonel out of his cage. Unfortunately, the boy who had been annoying the Colonel was in the room at the time. The Colonel leapt straight across the heads of all in the room and had to be hauled off the boy, but not until he had sunk his teeth into him. The damage had been done, not just to the boy but to the ongoing housing of animals, and all the animals had to be rehoused elsewhere.

In September 1963 when there was some doubt as to whether the Zoo would become a reality, an article listed some of the animals which were currently in temporary accommodation: badgers in England, foxes in St Andrews, three monkeys at Marischal College, donkeys at Hazlehead, ferrets in the Aberdeen Publicity office window, wallabies in Dundee, a seal in Shetland, an otter in Foula, monkeys in Dyce, goats in Garthdee and various macaws, cockatoos, grey parrot, six varieties of pheasant, capercaillie, native and tropical fish and, although not mentioned in the article, there were poisonous spiders and centipedes in Mastrick.

I cannot emphasise enough the contribution made by various people and organisations who gave up their time and provided food and homes to these animals. They met this expense out of their own pockets and deserve more recognition, as without their commitment the Zoo would have opened with a fraction of the exhibits that there were on display on that first day in July 1966.

The Zoo Project moves Forward

After my earlier comment on the lack of credibility of the initial budgets, it was in September 1962 that the City Architect, George Keith, tabled the first official budget of £40,000 to build the 'Little Zoo' based on the zoo nucleus at Hazlehead. This proposed layout was planned in June 1962 and included an enclosure for kangaroos and wallabies, demonstrating that Aberdeen City Council always envisaged housing more exotic animals, in addition to Scottish indigenous species both current and extinct. These included wolves, bison, beaver and lynx which are the animals many are proposing to 'rewild' the UK.

As my father became more involved with the Society, including organising the farming-out of animals and generally assisting with the travelling shows, he was appointed as Curator of Equipment in October 1962. It is perhaps worthy of note that my father was still employed as a hospital porter and assistant post-mortem attendant right up to his appointment as Manager of the Zoo in October 1966. It is fair to say that outside his 9.00 to 5.00 job he was working flat out to help make the Zoo a reality.

Dr Lil de Kock encapsulated the thoughts behind the formation of the Zoo in an article reprinted in the Aberdeen University Review, Vol. XXXIX, 4, No.128, pp.323-324, Autumn 1962.

A Zoological Garden for Aberdeen

In December 1961 the Aberdeen and North of Scotland Zoological Society was formed with Professor V.C. Wynne-Edwards as its first President, Professor T.C. Phemister and the Lord Provost of Aberdeen – Professor J.M. Graham - as Vice Presidents, and Mr Peter Scott as Adviser. The Society is the seventh Zoological Society in Great Britain.

The Constitution of the newly formed Society expresses the wishes of its founders to create a zoological garden in which only those animals will be kept which will thrive and breed in captivity, and which can be kept under the most natural conditions. Further, the Society aims at close cooperation with the Schools of Aberdeen and the surrounding districts, since it hopes to support the schools in many ways by facilitating the teaching of biology and thereby to raise the children's understanding of and love of nature and encourage the child to be interested in its preservation.

From the very beginning the Society's relations with the town have been cordial and close, in fact close negotiations have taken place as to the possibility of the town's assistance with the financing of the zoological garden in Aberdeen; indeed, at present, there is every hope of the Society opening the first section of the Zoo in the summer of 1963. The site envisaged is ideal - adjacent to the newly re-built restaurant at Hazlehead- with excellent transport facilities and all essential services already laid on.

A number of unusual and novel ideas have been incorporated in the planned buildings for housing the actual exhibits, and in this the staff of the City Architect's Department showed outstanding help and understanding; for example, there will be a beehive, large enough to take twenty-five people inside it. In it the bees' busy activities can be closely watched through the glass walls, their sounds will be transmitted to the observer and special bees will be marked to help the public get an understanding of the high social organization of the bee community. There will also be demonstrations of honey-extraction and bottling so that the visitor will be able to see for himself the making of the famous 'Scottish Honey', in a most fascinating way.

In connection with another exhibit, the observer will have to descend into an outsize molehill where, under a dim red light, he will be able to watch moles at work, together with a number of other subterranean creatures.

The Insect House - in the shape of a giant beetle - will contain not only a large number of insects and other invertebrates - some of them of great medical importance - but also a beautiful exhibit of free-flying exotic butterflies amidst tropical flowers, all brilliantly illuminated-a real stimulant on a dull November afternoon! One end of the Insect house will have a cinema to seat fifty people. A very recently developed type of microscope will throw an image on to a screen in full colour of whatever is under the microscope. The audience will thus be easily introduced to the sub-microscopic world with all its weird and wonderful forms. This should be especially useful to the Biology teacher and a great help in teaching.

In the Nocturnal House, the visitor will be gradually led from daylight to 'moon-lit' exhibits. Animals, normally asleep during daytime can be changed from night to a day activity by night illumination and semi-darkness during the day. The inside of the Nocturnal house will be rather similar to a planetarium; the dim light emerging from behind the silhouette of Aberdeen. The ceiling will show the monthly constellation of the Aberdeen night sky.

In other buildings the theme of evolution of the animal kingdom will be illustrated, an idea which was suggested by Mr Scott, and which was already realized for 'dead' animal exhibits in the Natural History Museum in Marischal College - the lay-out of this excellent Museum was beautifully designed by Professor Hardy, while holding the Chair of Natural History in Aberdeen.

The *Aberdeen Zoo* will also hold enclosures for the more exciting animals such as bears, antelopes, a full collection of native mammals, present and extinct (in Scotland), and of birds and monkeys. But the procuring of some of these exhibits will have to await the second development plan which provides for the final size of the Zoo being approximately 10 acres.

The Society's other activity will be devoted to education. A detailed programme has already been worked out in conjunction with the Education Authorities for lectures, demonstrations and junior meetings, and for the temporary loan of animals to schools. Many schools have helped greatly in the enrolment of our junior members and the distribution of membership badges and have co-operated in the organization of meetings in Marischal College. At such meetings films, lectures and exhibits of live animals are arranged. In addition, an advisory body of experts is available to advise on the different animal groups, a book club has been formed, and several educational pamphlets dealing with the care of pets, and giving some interesting information on origin, habitat and behaviour of the animals are free to members.

The response and enthusiasm of the youngsters proved to be a worthwhile effort, although slightly overwhelming-more than 1,000 children attended the first meeting! This satisfactory state of affairs does not, unfortunately, apply to the three categories of senior memberships which are available, although the Society's activities will naturally depend entirely on strong support from the more 'substantial' adult members.

The junior members are grouped into units of 24, the 25th being the Society's 'representative' at schools. The representatives receive a free badge and act as liaison between the schools, the Society and the group. Special representative meetings are arranged from time to time. The membership of juniors is, at the time of writing, 1,400, with new members coming in steadily. The Society takes this as a sign that the children of this area are only too pleased to have, indeed are in need of, a focus for their love and interest in animals in the form of a Zoological Garden in Aberdeen.

L. L. de Kock

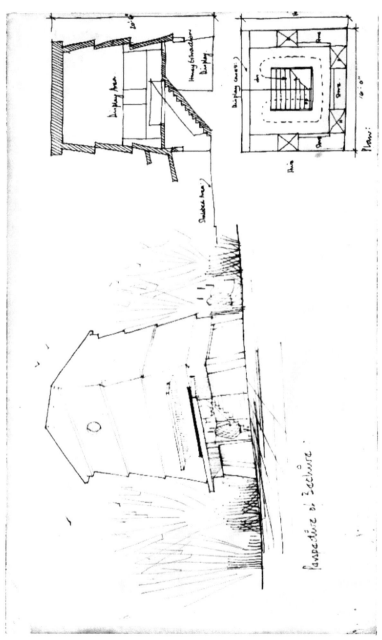

Perspective of Beehive

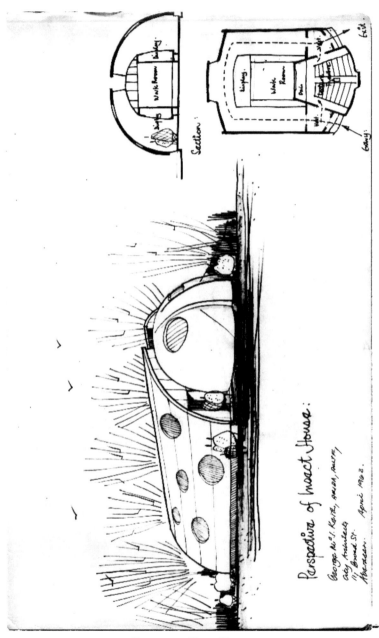

Perspective of Insect House

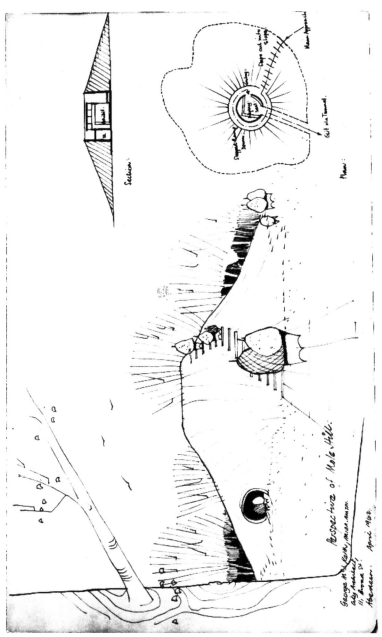

Perspective of Mole Hill

24

Perspective of Monkey House

25

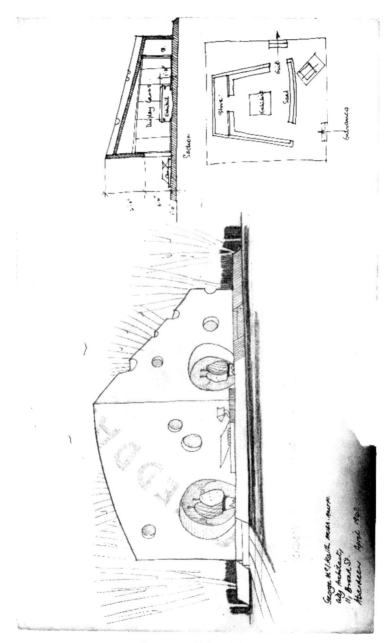

Perspective of Mouse Town

26

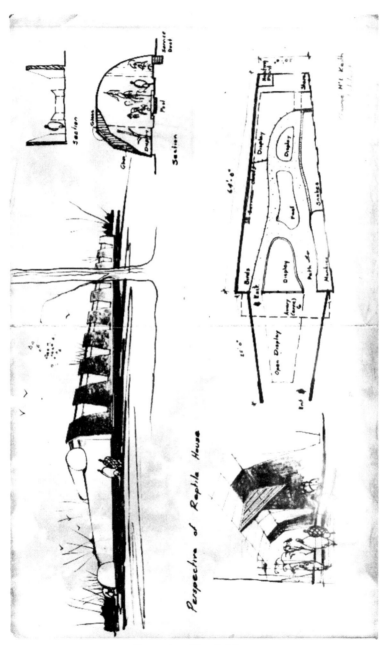

Perspective of Reptile House

27

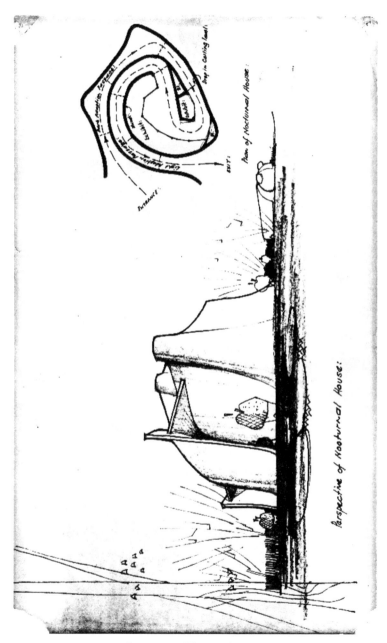

Perspective of Nocturnal House

The plans also envisaged the expansion into the rugby pitches and the miniature golf. By November 1962 the Society's plans showed the initial two-acre site east of the Hazlehead Restaurant and a further 10-12 acres of expansion.

In the early years there were various predictions as to the possible attendance, income etc., but it is clear there were very many unknowns as there were no data of similar enterprises to give any guidance.

By January 1963 Aberdeen City Council was willing to expend £28,000 in erecting the first phase of the Zoo, to lease the land at an economic rent, guarantee any loss during the first three years to a maximum of £1,000 in any one year, and to consider the second phase when the first phase had been in operation for not less than one year. In November 1963 the Council approved a loan of £30,500 for the Zoo. It is fair to say that there was not unanimous support for the Zoo. Councillor J.S.G. Munro is reported as saying '*I think the Zoo is a waste of time and money. The money would be better spent in the beach development which has been talked about for years*'. However, by September 1964 Lord Provost Norman Hogg saw fit to promise Aberdeen City Council's wholehearted support.

As all these plans were being progressed, I note that much of the correspondence from Aberdeen City Council appeared to focus on the conditions of employment of the zookeepers and how much the Zoo intended paying them. A cynical person may think that Aberdeen City Council was concerned about losing employees from Links and Parks to the Zoo enterprise.

Interestingly, the Progress Report included the minutes of the first Annual General Meeting held on 28th May 1963, which noted that the choice of site at Hazlehead of two and a half acres was too small for effective development. Further, it was recorded that 'delays have caused the Society to consider a Wildlife Park outside the city'. With this in mind, Lil de Kock wrote to the Aberdeenshire Planning Officer to ask whether he could give a decision, in principle, to the creation of a Wildlife Park at Lochhead of Leys, Banchory, as she was minded to acquire 88 acres of farmland laying astride the Banchory/Raemoir Road. As a result of another enquiry a response was received from the owners of the Mar Lodge Estate. There is a letter from G.S. Panchaud written from Lausanne stating, '*A nature reserve on the Mar Lodge Estate after the style of Whipsnade might well be possible*'. There is also correspondence which shows a linkage with a Wildlife Park near Aviemore, enquiries being sent to the Rothiemurcus Estate with a view to establish a park which would be managed by the Society. None of these alternative sites materialised and the decisions to locate the Zoo at Hazlehead had a huge influence on the project.

As the choice of location was to have such an impact on the future of the Zoo, it is worth taking time to allocate the next three sections to the timeline regarding the location and expansion of the Zoo, otherwise the impact of this one factor on the subsequent Elephant Fund and the final fate of the Zoo would be lost.

Location

The Zoo was located at Hazlehead, where the Pets Corner is located today – but the choice of location was not a foregone conclusion.

As previously mentioned, in January 1963 Aberdeen City Council was willing to expend £28,000 in erecting the first phase of the Zoo. Mr Winning, who was the head of Links and Parks in Aberdeen, was very keen on the concept of the Zoo and I remember images of Hazlehead showing the future phases of the Zoo and the park. The plan was to expand the Zoo into Hazlehead Park and create a weekend destination for the families of Aberdeen.

With this plan in mind, the Society set up a working group to establish Invertebrate and Tropical Houses, (to be constructed from Romney-type huts), an Entrance Building, Toilet Facilities and a Keeper's House.

Lil de Kock (centre) and her assistant discuss the plans with the City Architect's Department

Support from Aberdeen City Council was not unanimous, and this forced the committee to keep looking for alternative sites to Hazlehead. To this end the committee prepared an advertisement for a site of between 5 and 10 acres within a 25-mile radius of Aberdeen.

Aberdeen City Council offered a two-acre site at Hazlehead in May 1963, but at a high cost. The committee considered various alternatives at Tornaveen, Crathes Castle, Delgatie Castle at Turriff, Williamston House at Colpy, Invercauld Estate and a Royal Northern Agricultural farm at the Bridge of Don. There is even a record of land at Garthdee Road and Seaton Park being investigated, but these were both discounted. Eventually it was felt that declining the site at Hazlehead would alienate Aberdeen City Council and it was agreed to proceed with this site.

In 1963 it was recorded that the Zoo would not be ready until 1965, but a proposal for a temporary zoo at sites at Tillycorthie or Banchory was rejected.

Geoff Stevens overseeing the construction

By October 1964 drawings had been progressed by the City Architect's Department and showed the Zoo Manager's three-bedroom detached house, an Exhibition House, Tropical House and aviary. Enclosures were also planned for donkeys, wallabies and kangaroos, small deer and antelopes, and a children's corner was designed.

After much consultation with the main parties it is clear from the plans drawn up that, rather than the original concept of the Zoo, it would include non-indigenous animals.

In addition, correspondence from The Rowett Institute included hopes that exhibits of sheep and cattle from Mediterranean and African areas, African wild ruminants and a selection of marsupials, especially herbivores, be included.

The Zoo Project progressed on this basis and opened in July 1966.

Lil de Kock, Mum and Dad - all hands to the pump as the opening date grows near

Children's Corner takes shape

Plans for Extension

In March 1967 it was noted in the minutes of the Society's meeting that Lil de Kock was to leave Aberdeen to work with the world-famous zoologist, Dr Konrad Lorenz, at his research institute near Munich. At this point, Basil Parrish took over as Convener.

During 1967 the expansion of the Zoo was considered, first to the north of the existing Zoo utilising a pedestrian bridge. By May 1967 the Town Planning Department favoured expansion into Hazlehead Park, in keeping with the original vision.

But there was still opposition to the concept of the Zoo. Mr Winning was replaced as Director of Links and Parks by David Welch, who clearly did not subscribe to the original concept.

The first stage in the expansion of the Zoo into the area occupied by the potting sheds had been promised for some time. However, progress on this was positively glacial, which affected many plans, in particular the infamous Elephant Fund.

In 1967 opposition to the Zoo was noted in the Council minutes and the Society was being asked to consider a 100-acre farmland site adjacent to Aberdeen, but this was too costly to proceed.

Around this time (the document is undated) Basil Parrish tabled a fairly concise report on the situation with regard to the problem of the Zoo's extension and I have transcribed it in its entirety as it gives not only the details of the problems but also a flavour of the frustrations being felt by the Zoo's management.

Notes on the Problem of the Zoo Extension

Recapitulation of Past Policy

It has been the Society's declared policy from the beginning that the present Zoo constitutes only the first phase of a substantially larger development, involving an increase in its size to at least two or three times the present acreage. This was to allow an increase in the number and range of exhibits and the provision of larger, open enclosures, especially for the 'hoofed' species.

In its early consideration of this expansion (termed Phase B), the additional area which the Council had in mind was the pitch and putt course on the north side of the present site. This had been suggested by the then Director of Links and Parks. This site does, however, suffer a number of deficiencies, especially:

(a) it would necessitate having to cross the road

(b) it possesses no natural landscaping

Therefore, attention was subsequently directed towards alternative areas of expansion, particularly within the main park. This was prompted by views expressed by the Town Planning Officer, who considered that the area from the park entrance to about the level of the bandstand would constitute a very suitable, landscaped area for expansion.

In general, the Council became enthusiastic about this alternative and preferred it to the pitch and putt course, and it became the focal point of the Management Committee's consideration of future plans. An important feature of the Council's and the Town Planning Officer's thinking was that this area was large enough to meet the Zoo's needs in the foreseeable future, as well as providing an attractive and readily accessible site. Moreover, it was considered that a Zoo of this size was a practicable, economic proposition, necessitating no radical changes in its administration and financial control.

Recent Developments

This thinking persisted until very recently when the new Director of Links and Parks, Mr Welch, took up office. He made it known that he was strongly opposed to the Council's policy of extending into the main park (and indeed also into the pitch and putt course area) on the following grounds: -

(a) The area of the park in question is too valuable as a public amenity in its present form.

(b) The size of Zoo which could be developed on this basis would be too small (i) to allow the number of animals displayed to increase sufficiently to meet the inevitable (and desirable) needs in the future, (ii) to permit the provision of enclosures of a desirable size and layout, to comply with the Council's declared policy of an 'open' type of display.

In his view the future requirements justify a site of around 50 acres which would allow a satisfactory mixture of large and small enclosures according to the needs of different types of exhibits. There are sites meeting these requirements on farmland, owned by the Town Council on the outskirts of the city. Mr Welch is of the view that the Town Council should be approached to make such a 50-acre site available. In his view, once the larger Zoo had become established (but not necessarily fully developed) the present Zoo site could perhaps be converted into a children's Zoo and become part of the public amenities of Hazlehead Park.

In subsequent discussions with Mr Welch and the Town Planning Officer it has become clear that the latter has been won over to Mr Welch's view of the situation and is also advocating that serious thought be given to this larger expansion. Both have expressed the opinion that Aberdeen and the north-east of Scotland represent a sufficiently large centre of population and holiday and tourist area to provide an adequate visiting public to support a '50-acre' type zoo (as distinct from a 5-10 acre one).

Questions facing the Council

Although it is possible that Mr Welch could, under sufficient strength of argument, be persuaded to change his present attitude towards this problem (if he did I think the Town Planning Officer would also do so), I am sure that he will not do so lightly (he is quite sincere in his present judgement of the situation and is in no sense setting out to kill the Zoo; indeed, he has pledged himself a very keen 'Zoo' man. Therefore, I think the Council has no alternative but to give very serious consideration to his proposals.

The principal questions which we have to consider can perhaps be posed as follows: -

(1) Given the necessary capital outlay could a Zoo in Aberdeen, of the size envisaged by Mr Welch, be viable economically? (By viable economically I mean that the revenue from all sources would be sufficiently in excess of total costs including payments of rental charges, depreciation on buildings etc., to provide adequate funds for replacement of exhibits and site developments).

The answer to this key question involves, of course, an assessment of both the revenue which might be expected and the total costs. I think the first off-the-cuff answer which one is most likely to give this question is 'no' (it was certainly my first reaction), but I'm sure we must try to make a more detailed assessment of it. We probably do not have sufficient, relevant information to make the assessment from our own activities since the Zoo opened, so, we must seek the information from elsewhere. I think we should tackle the assessment from the cost end first, by obtaining from one or two well established zoos of an appropriate size in this country as detailed a breakdown as possible of their total costs. This should permit us to make some reasonably objective estimates of the total annual revenue which we must raise to break-even financially and, in particular, the required income from gate receipts. We could then use this estimate as a basis for judging whether the 'catchment area' in the NE of Scotland is large enough.

(2) If the answer to question (1) is in the affirmative, can the necessary capital funds be found to launch the larger Zoo?

It seems to me that there are two possible sources of capital for the development of the Zoo site (erection of buildings, landscaping, etc.) and the purchase of animals: -

(a) the Town Council

(b) Private fundraising and loans

I think that we should reckon on money being obtained from both sources, the Town Council putting up the necessary capital for the main essentials for the site development and fundraising the money for animal purchases etc. The Society would need to launch a vigorous, local fundraising campaign, perhaps with the assistance of professional, fundraising services. I can see no objective way by which we can assess in advance the success of such a campaign, but the rate of development of the programme could be geared to the situation at the time.

(3) What sort and size of Management and staffing organisation would be required for a zoo of this size?

(4) Can an adequate site, situated sufficiently close to the city, on a public transport route be acquired?

(5) If the answer to questions (1)-(3) are all answered satisfactorily in the affirmative, does the Society consider that it should pursue the idea and if so, what sort of timetable should be followed?

My own view of the problem as a whole is that we should go ahead with as detailed an assessment of questions (1)-(3) as we can make, but that we should do it on the basis that a zoo of the present size (including the promised, small extension into the potting shed area) is not doomed to failure and can, if adequately maintained, continue to thrive and meet the needs of the population of the north-east of Scotland.

B. Parrish

As you will see in the section on the Elephant Fund, the decision on whether to have an elephant hinged on the availability of additional land and a letter was written to Norman McPhee of the Evening Express in September 1969 confirming Aberdeen City Council had not made the area of the potting sheds available. The

Society also saw fit to confirm that the Zoo paid £2,490, a full economic rent, to Aberdeen City Council and did not receive any contribution towards the running costs, to allay any suggestions that the Zoo was in some way subsidised by Aberdeen City Council.

By 1971 Aberdeen City Council was investigating the separate development of a Country Park. In 1972 the Links and Parks Committee reported that they would not let the Zoo have additional land.

A change of mind was noted in 1973 by Aberdeen City Council as the potting sheds were offered, but the use had to be acceptable to Aberdeen City Council. At this time, it can be surmised from the minutes that things were beginning to unravel with requests for the larger animals to be transferred to help Aberdeen City Council establish a Country Park. There was even a suggestion that the caravan site could be used to exhibit small animals.

During my research into the history of the Zoo, I came across a response from the Town Clerk regarding the additional land. In a hand-written postscript he stated, off the record, that he was sympathetic to the Zoo, and was upset that Aberdeen City Council had reneged on its promises regarding the extension.

In 1974 Aberdeen City Council requested information from the Society about farming out some animals, and asked for a sketch map of a replacement Zoo to help cut down noise and smell.

Another change of mind was noted with Aberdeen City Council offering the potting sheds, but with the condition that this was changed to a children's play area.

By 1975 Dr Bob Ralph, the Secretary of the Society, was really frustrated by the situation and wrote to Ian Maclure (Depute Director of Law and Administration) stating *'It is obvious that there is some hardening opposition from the Town towards the Zoo in its present form and the Society cannot satisfactorily continue with such a bad relationship'*.

In 1976 the pressure was ramped up on the Zoo to only stock small indigenous animals. To try and elicit a way forward Professor Salzen, the final Convener of the Society, sent a letter dated 15th March 1976 to David Welch enclosing a list of animals and requesting the list be marked up to show animals unsuitable for a Zoo receiving the backing and financial support from Aberdeen City Council. There is no record of a response being received.

In a further effort to break the deadlock and identify a way forward which would be acceptable to both parties, an informal meeting was held. The date of this meeting is unrecorded, but the Zoo was represented by Dr Bob Ralph and my father, Aberdeen City Council was represented by Councillors Collie, Lennox and Mutch, and also present were David Welch, Representatives of Planning, Engineering and City Chamberlain. The agenda covered:

1) Problem of the Zoo as it stands
2) Disputes regarding extra area at Hazlehead
3) Relocation of the Zoo

It appears that the Town needed assurances that the Zoo had no plans or ideas of expanding further at Hazlehead beyond the disputed area. They were given this assurance.

The matter of a Country Park to the south of the River Dee where some of the larger animals could be relocated was also raised. It was suggested that this would allow more green areas in the existing Zoo. I personally find this a peculiar comment, as the Zoo was adjacent to the big green space which was Hazlehead Park.

As I look back, I cannot help but think what might have been achieved with a bit of collaboration.

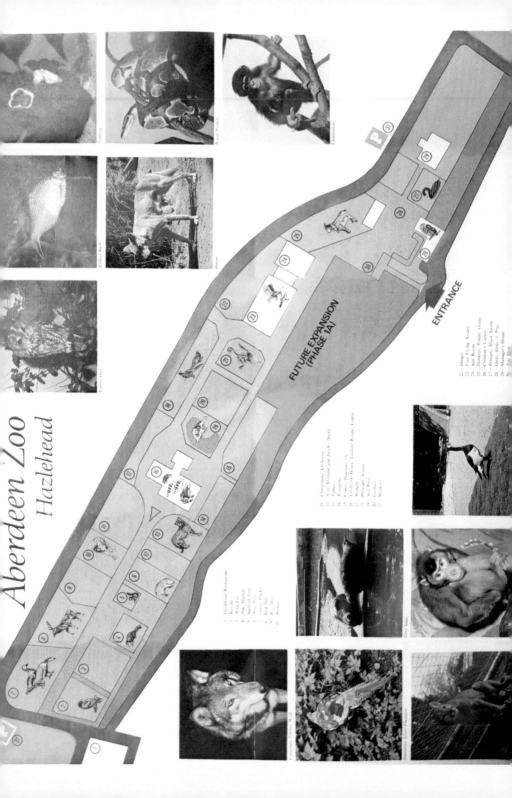

Aberdeen Zoo
Hazlehead

ENTRANCE

FUTURE EXPANSION
(PHASE 1A)

1 Hazlehead Restaurant
2 Bison
3 Wild Cat
4 Pine Marten
5 Squirrel Cage
6 Wild Pig
7 Geese, Ducks
8 Red Deer
9 Red Deer
10 Wolves

11 Champagne Enclosure
12 Scottish Wildcat and Jacob's Sheep
13 Pathos
14 Porcupine
15 Cattle, Peacocks, etc.
16 Children's House, Lecture Room, Toilets
17 Wallaby
18 Pheasant, Black Swans
19 Seal Pool
20 Grebes
21 Monkey

22 Dingo
23 Free Flying Aviary
24 Sun Room
25 Donkeys, Ponies, Goats
26 Children's Corner
27 Penguins, Black Swans
28 Owls, Birds of Prey
29 Manager's House
30 Zoo Shop

Aberdeen Zoo becomes a Reality

Geoff Stevens and young seal

Some people thought that my father was the first manager of the Zoo, but in actual fact Geoff Stevens was appointed as the first Zoo Manager. Geoffrey William Stevens was manager of Southport Zoo before taking up the position of Manager at Aberdeen Zoo. Geoff had started his career as a reporter in Sheffield and became an Assistant Editor at Newton Chambers and Co. Ltd. He then moved to Borneo and during his time as the Organising Commissioner for boy scouts in Sarawak, Sabah and Brunei he accumulated a small private collection of animals. I presume that Geoff took this collection to Southport Zoo. He brought his collection of animals to Aberdeen and they were housed in the Zoo.

I do not know why things did not work out with Geoff, but his resignation was accepted in the second half of 1966 and my father was offered the post of Manager. He took up the position on 1st October 1966, on the princely salary of £1,000/annum reducing to £800/annum when we took occupation of the house.

I do not remember much about Geoff other than he had a very large Alsatian dog called Khan and, on our first meeting, I reached out my hand to shake Geoff's when he warned me against it as Khan would probably see his master in imminent danger and attack me. Once you got to know Khan he was alright, but I remember being left in the house with him as he paced back and forth and kept giving me the evil eye. This was not the most comfortable hour of my life!

During the summer of 1966 there were a lot of alterations and additional fencing to be done and I remember that Geoff's brother, Roger, came up to Aberdeen to help. Roger was a real joker and I remember him cracking joke after joke as we tried to wield pickaxes and post hammers with tears of laughter running down our faces.

The Society had cooperated with Aberdeen City Council to finance this, but this was to be the first phase of a larger project. Plans were in hand for a further phase, and it was hoped that the Zoo would continue to develop both as a tourist attraction and a local amenity.

Back in 1962 Peter Scott, the renowned naturalist and artist, had established the Wildfowl & Wetlands Trust reserve at Slimbridge, and helped to found the World Wide Fund for Nature (WWF). He had noticed the proposals for a zoo in Aberdeen and had asked to be closely associated with the Zoo. Early in 1966 he had commented that Aberdeen was to be the most interesting zoo in the world. A zoo without bars, with an emphasis on Scottish animals, education and an informative labelling system. It was therefore inevitable that he was invited to write a short introduction for the Zoo Brochure.

As it became evident that the Zoo was to be a reality, and would open later that year, it was deemed prudent that the Zoo should become a Company limited by guarantee. The Company was set up in January 1966. The principal effect of the incorporation was to limit the liability of the full members of the Society to £1 in the event of the Company going into liquidation.

A list of the Signatories to the Memorandum and Articles of Association is attached as Appendix 2.

The Zoo opened on the 16th July, 1966.

Peter Scott was also invited to officiate at the opening of the Zoo. At the time he was the President of the WWF, and as I had designed a wishing well to accept donations for the Fund, I met him as he thanked me for my efforts.

OPENING OF ABERDEEN ZOO

The Lord Provost, Magistrates and Town Council of Aberdeen request the pleasure of the company of

at Luncheon in the Beach Ballroom Aberdeen on Saturday 16 July 1966 at 12.15 p.m. for 12.30 p.m., at which Mr. Peter Scott, C.B.E., D.S.C., will be the principal guest.

TOWN HOUSE,
ABERDEEN, July, 1966.

R.S.V.P. to the
Lord Provost's Secretary.

The official opening took place on 16th July 1966 and the list of those invited to the official opening lunch was quite impressive. They included the Lord Provost Norman Hogg, six Bailies, Deans of Guild, Treasurer Lennox, Town Clerk plus two Deputies, 11 Councillors, Director of Parks, City

Chamberlain, City Architect, Director of Publicity, officials from the WWF, and 12 others including the RT Hon Earl and Countess of Haddo and Lord and Lady Percy.

The Zoo was opened at 11.00am, the Wishing Well at 11.30am and the official lunch was held at the Beach Ballroom at 12.30 pm. Peter Scott then left and gave a lecture at the Music Hall at 2.00 pm.

In tandem with the official opening, my father decided to visit all the people who he considered had helped make the Zoo a reality. This celebration involved the consumption of quite a lot of whisky. The next day my father was at work at Aberdeen Royal Infirmary, where he unfortunately took ill. An ulcer had burst, but at least he was in the right place and was rushed into surgery. I think it is fair to say that he was very seriously ill and only survived thanks to the skill of the surgeons. During his recuperation he still attended the Zoo and was obviously well enough to be considered for the post of Manager later that year.

Opening of the Zoo

As you will see from the section 'How do you Measure Success' the Zoo had 10,000 visitors in the first two days. So many in fact, that in the first weekend the Zoo had to be closed to new entrants as there was a real concern for the safety of the public.

Peter Scott, Dad and Pierre de Kock at the opening of the Zoo

The Zoo went on to attract 30,000 visitors in the first two weeks.

I remember vividly the early days when I was helping out at the entrance gate during the first summer. The Zoo had two ticket windows, one at the shop side and the other a booth dedicated to the sale of tickets. After a couple of hours selling tickets and guide maps and counting out the change (remember there were no electronic cash registers and no pocket calculators), you were like a washed-out rag and literally fell out of the door when someone came to relieve you!

Mr Peter Scott with a Brahminy Kite at the opening of the Zoo

LINING UP FOR CITY'S NEWEST ATTRACTION

18th July 1966 – a few of the 10,000 people who flocked to Hazlehead to see Aberdeen's Zoo

Keeping the Cost Down

While the costs of staff wages and rent etc. to Aberdeen City Council were fixed, the costs that could be controlled were those of adaptations of the enclosures and of course food.

The wage bill was minimised using volunteer labour. Young boys and girls were desperate to work with animals. This brought with it some health and safety issues which I will touch on later. The reality was a rude awakening to some who had never had to muck out a stable, when cleaning the bottom of a budgie's cage was the extent of their experience. However, we were assisted by many fit and able youngsters who saved the cost of additional keepers.

More savings were made using off-duty firemen to construct new enclosures or adapt the existing ones. My father was very practical, and what he lacked in finesse he made up for by the 'belt and braces' approach, which usually involved the use of large timbers and many six-inch nails.

My father also utilised his farming upbringing and sourced many materials from farm roups or sales. Fencing posts and materials, wheelbarrows and tools were all procured in this way. The visits to these farm roups were an education. The farmers displayed the typical thrift which abounds in the North East of Scotland. Times were tough pre-North Sea oil and many were super resourceful - if you kept anything seven years, you would eventually find a use for it! This thrift was the norm, but there was some intense rivalry between farmers which led to overspending. As an example, on one occasion we needed some fence posts, but had not bargained on two farmers having an argument using the posts as the spoils of war! In the end the victor paid more than the new price for a pile of second-hand posts, but presumably went away happy.

In those days the auctioneer would set up an office in the farmhouse to take in the payments. No Apple Pay then; it was just cash or cheque. One day my father went to pay for an item and was away ages - he came back laughing. The chap in front of him had purchased the farmer's Volvo for £800+ and paid for it in cash, in one-pound notes which he insisted on counting out. Obviously, a man ahead of his time. He did not trust bankers, relying instead on the funds from the biscuit tin under the bed.

The other main cost was in animal feedstuffs. Again, my father's background resulted in him cutting out the middle-man and going direct to farmers for hay and vegetables.

Meat was a bit trickier. We took up the offer of condemned chickens from Grampian Country Chickens on Mugiemoss Road. The abattoir process involved live chickens being put on a conveyor belt at one end and fully packaged chickens ready for the supermarket shelves coming out the other. We were offered the chickens which were unfit for human consumption as they had fallen off the conveyor belt after being killed.

On many a Friday afternoon I would head to Mugiemoss Road to pick up plastic sacks filled with chickens, which were bundled into the trailer and taken back to Hazlehead. Again, it reflects a different time with different regulations, but sometimes we were called to Aberdeen Mart at Kittybrewster. Here animals, mainly sheep, which had been badly hurt during transportation, were humanely dispatched. These were used to feed the dingoes, wolves, pumas and lions. It is a wonder I did not turn vegetarian at this point in my life when I experienced the sights and smells of these carcasses. Fresh meat did not bother me, but I still remember the revulsion when shifting an old carcass from the dingoes to find it writhing with maggots.

The smaller carnivores and reptiles needed either day-old chicks or mice in their diet and again, using his farming and hospital connections, my father purchased day-old chicks from the Mart when there was a surplus. These were taken to the Zoo where they were dispatched and kept in the freezer. Likewise, mice which were surplus to requirements at the Medical School were given to the Zoo, where they too were dispatched and kept to feed the snakes and birds of prey.

Let's quickly move on to fruit! The old Rover 90 and trailer were in action at least twice a week as we visited what is now Asda at the Bridge of Dee. The Manager had offered to put aside any bruised or rotten fruit and vegetables from his stock. Sometimes there would be only one or two pieces of damaged fruit in each pack and these were sorted out back at the Zoo. As a result, the animals enjoyed perfectly good fruit.

All of the above helped to keep costs down and were probably instrumental in keeping the Zoo going, particularly during the winter period when only the hardiest of visitors would brave the elements.

Publicity

The Zoo always attracted interest from the people of the North East of Scotland and Aberdeen Journals supplied the conduit for disseminating the latest ongoing sagas.

In the early years Aberdeen Journals reported on runaway animals from our home in Sheddocksley Road, before turning its attention to similar escapes from the actual Zoo. Aberdeen Journals also carried reports on the phenomenal attendance figures in the first couple of weeks. The forthcoming Senior and Junior Zoo Club events were well covered in the press, and you could not fault them for taking a very positive view of the Zoo.

Once the Zoo became a physical reality Aberdeen Journals was very supportive, carrying comments from Peter Scott that the Zoo was one of the most interesting in the world because of its emphasis on indigenous Scottish animals and emphasising the educational resource that the Zoo supplied. Equally it also reported that Peter Scott was unimpressed by Aberdeen City's £25,000 loan to the Zoo, citing the example of the Isle of Man government, which gave £45,000 to assist a much

Prof. Eric Salzen, Dad and John Buchan (with Lass, the Wolf) at Shell receiving a donation from Mr Fred Chate

smaller project on the island.

Aberdeen Journals was always keen to explore ways of linking local stories to the Zoo, and in July 1966 they carried the story of local girl Irene Blues, who had been chosen to ride a Billy Smart's Circus elephant at the head of the procession from Aberdeen Station to the showground where the circus had set up. The relevant connection was that Irene was about to take up a post as a Junior Keeper at the Zoo.

The Journals certainly kept the levels of interest up with articles about many of the animals housed at the Zoo from agoutis to Vietnamese pot-bellied pigs. (I am only sorry we didn't have zebras to make it an A to Z!). It was not only the Zoo which derived publicity from the animals. The numerous cinemas in Aberdeen were keen to have props to publicise the latest release, from 'Where Eagles Dare' to 'Born Free'. Other ventures also donated money for the use of tame animals from the Zoo.

For example, the Beachcomber Bar and Restaurant at the Gloucester Hotel on Union Street borrowed a few exotic birds and animals to add interest to their grand opening.

Geoff Ramsden and Dad with 'Tweet' the Eagle publicising the opening of 'Where Eagles Dare'

As mentioned earlier, I was surprised at how public the disagreements between the Zoo and Aberdeen Council were regarding the ongoing wrangle over the area of the potting sheds. I would say that the press took a pro Zoo stance throughout the life of the Zoo and even when derogatory comments were being made by various elected Councillors, the press were rooting for the Zoo.

Enjoy a visit

to

ABERDEEN

ZOO

THE ANIMALS & BIRDS HAVE
BEEN SELECTED TO DELIGHT
CHILDREN AND ADULTS ALIKE!
OPEN DAILY from 10 a.m. - 9 p.m.

Admission: Adults 2/6; Juniors 1/3; Children under 3, free.

SPECIAL RATES FOR ORGANISED PARTIES

Pensioners 1/-   (Members Free)

Hazlehead Park, Aberdeen

No. 4 BUS TO TERMINUS

April Fools' Day

An unexpected resource problem occurred some nine months after the Zoo opened. It started first thing in the morning with the phone ringing. '*Can I speak to Mr C. Lion*', followed by other calls to Mr Albert Ross. It was of course the first of April. The phone calls were constant all morning requiring a member of staff to sit by the phone fending off calls for Mr G. Raff.

Some of the callers became quite indignant as they could not be connected and out of embarrassment at being conned by their friends and colleagues. The Zoo provided an outlet for the April Fools' jibes, and every year a member of staff was stationed by the phone to fend off all the calls. If of course the caller seemed particularly obnoxious, he or she was asked to hold while someone was sent to round up Mr Lion or Mr Humphrey.

Staff & Volunteers

I have mentioned the staff a few times throughout this history of the Zoo, but it is worth underlining the great contribution they made in running the Zoo. In my experience, they were all dedicated to providing care for the animals in their charge, above and beyond their contractual hours.

Denise Dempster with MacNicol

It was not unusual for keepers to stay with any of their animals which were sick until they had nursed them back to full fitness.

The Zoo was initially staffed by one Head Keeper and three Junior Keepers, but it was also acknowledged that part-time and volunteer labour would be required to carry out all the necessary duties.

Dennis Milne, who had been an animal technician at the University of Aberdeen's Animal House at Foresterhill, was interviewed and chosen as the first Head Keeper.

The Keepers had a busy schedule. It was not all about sitting and cuddling cute furry little animals; there was a list of tasks to assist them keep track of their duties on a weekly basis. Attached are the schedules for the Top Section, Aviary Section and the Children's Corner to give a flavour of the weekly chores.

(left to right) - Iain Morrice, John Buchan, James Forrest and Denise Dempster

Example of the daily rota for the Top Section

TOP SECTION.

	8:30 - 11:30	11:30 - LUNCH	LUNCH - 4:30	4:30 - 5:30	FEEDING
MONDAY	CHECK ALL ANIMALS. FEED CHIMPS. GIVE HAY + STRAW. SWEEP UP. GIVE FRESH WATER. REMOVE ALL FOOD TRAYS + CLEAN. CLEAN UP FAECES + DEBRI.	FEED ALL ANIMALS. CLEAN GLASS. ETC.		THOROUGH CLEAN DEER + OTTER ENCLOSURES	SWEEP PATHS. HELP TIDY STORE. EMPTY + WASH ALL WASTE BINS	CHIMPS - FRUIT, BREAD, GREENS TWICE DAILY. MACAQUES) FRUIT, BREAD, GREENS GIBBON) DAILY CATS) MEAT OR MRNS +A PINE MARTEN) CHICKS DAILY. RAVENS OWLS OTTERS - MEAT, MEWS, CHICKS OR FISH DAILY. (INCLUDING SUNDAY) DEER) HAY AT ALL TIMES LLAMA) CAKE/GRASS WHEN AVAILABLE ALLIGATOR - MEAT DAILY SNAKES - MICE, ETC WHEN NECESSARY. BUSH BABY - FRUIT, BREAD DAILY TOADS LIZARDS TORTOISES
TUESDAY	"	"		THOROUGH CLEAN CATS, PIGEONS, EAGLE, OWL + PINE MARTEN ENCLOSURES	"	
WEDNESDAY	"	"		THOROUGH CLEAN EXHIBITION HOUSE ENCLOSURES.	"	
THURSDAY	"	"		THOROUGH CLEAN MACAQUE + GIBBON ENCLOSURES	'	
FRIDAY	"	"		THOROUGH CLEAN CHIMP ENCLOSURE, SCRUB DOWN WALLS + LEDGES.	'	
SATURDAY	"	"		THOROUGH CLEAN PELICAN ENCLOSURE	'	
SUNDAY	"	"		THOROUGH CLEAN EXHIBITION HOUSE ENCLOSURES	'	MEAT EATERS NOT FED ON SUNDAY

51

AVIARY SECTION

	8:30 – 11:30	11:30 – LUNCH	LUNCH – 4:30	4:30 – 5:30	FEEDING
MONDAY	CHECK ALL ANIMALS, GIVE HAY + STRAW + SWEEP UP. GIVE FRESH WATER. REMOVE ALL FOOD	FEED ANIMALS + BIRDS + TIDY SECTION. CLEAN GLASS + WINDOW LEDGES	CLEAN KITCHEN, THOROUGH CLEAN NOCTURNAL EXHIBITS.	SWEEP PATHS. HELP TIDY STORE	SEALS – FISH AT 11:30 + 3:30 DAILY.
TUESDAY	TRAYS + CLEAN CLEAN UP FAECES + DEBRI	"	THOROUGH CLEAN WOLVES. SCRUB SEAL POOL	EMPTY + WASH ALOE WASTE BINS	WOLVES – MEAT ▓▓▓ AS REQUIRED PUMAS – "
WEDNESDAY	:	:	THOROUGH CLEAN BEAR ENCLOSURE + SLEEPING HUT. CLEAN. GUANACO PADDOCK	:	BEARS – FRUIT, BREAD, DAILY KINKAJOU } FRUIT, BREAD DAILY. PALM CIVET } CHICKS OCCASIONALLY
THURSDAY	:	:	THOROUGH CLEAN PHEASANT AVIARIES	:	BADGER } MEAT (VARIED), BREAD RACCOON } DAILY
FRIDAY	:	:	THOROUGH CLEAN PUMAS. SCRUB SEAL POOL	:	SQUIRRELS – FRUIT, NUTS, BREAD. GUANACO – HAY AT ALL TIMES. ROOT VEG WHEN AVAILABLE GREENS OCCASIONALLY
SATURDAY	:	:	THOROUGH CLEAN AVIARY, SEATS PERCHES, ETC. + POOL	:	PHEASANT – PELLETS IN HOPPERS AT ALL TIMES PARROTS – SUNFLOWER SEED. ETC. FRUIT, BREAD CRUMBS DAILY
SUNDAY	:	:	THOROUGH CLEAN PARROT AVIARY + POOL	:	AVIARY BIRDS – SEED + FRUIT DAILY CRANES – MINCED MEAT OR CHICKS WHOLE MAIZE OCCASIONALLY (CHEWING) FLAMINGOES – CYAMBED WHEAT + FLAMINGO DIET. MEAT EATERS NOT FED ON SUNDAY

Example of the daily rota for the Children's Corner

CHILDREN'S CORNER

	8.30 - 11.30	11.30 - Lunch	Lunch - 4.30	4.30 - 5.30	FEEDING
MONDAY	CHECK ALL ANIMALS. GIVE HAY + STRAW. SWEEP UP. GIVE FRESH WATER. REMOVE FOOD TRAYS	FEED ALL ANIMALS. TIDY SECTION.	THOROUGH CLEAN PADDOCK, INCLUDING SLEEPING HUTS.	SWEEP PATHS. HELP TIDY STORE. EMPTY + WASH ALL WASTE BINS	LLAMA) HAY AT ALL TIMES. GOATS) GREENS WHEN AVAILABLE ETC.) BREAD " "
TUESDAY	+ CLEAN. CLEAN UP FAECES + DEBRI	"	THOROUGH CLEAN POOL AND SURROUNDING AREA.	"	RABBITS) GREENS WHEN AVAILABLE G.PIGS) BREAD " ") OR TURNIP
WEDNESDAY	"	"	THOROUGH CLEAN HAWK, OWL, FOX + CIVET ENCLOSURES. (SCRUB BARRELS)	"	GEESE) BROKEN BREAD DAILY. DUCKS) PELLETS IN HOPPER AT SWANS) ALL TIMES.
THURSDAY	"	"	THOROUGH CLEAN RABBITS. RAKE SAND PIT. CLEAN BUDGERIGAR ENCLOSURE	"	BADGERS) MEAT FOX) OR DAILY OWLS) CHICKS HAWKS) LIONS) MEAT " CIVETS - MEAT, CHICKS, OR SCRAPS WITH A LITTLE FRUIT DAILY.
FRIDAY	"	"	THOROUGH CLEAN POOL AND SURROUNDING AREA	"	
SATURDAY	"	"	THOROUGH CLEAN CASSOWARY ENCLOSURE	"	BUDGERIGARS - SEED DAILY. GREENS + FRUIT WHEN AVAILABLE
SUNDAY	"	"	THOROUGH CLEAN DINGO ENCLOSURE	"	CASSOWARY - FRUIT, BREAD, GREENS TWICE DAILY. CHICKS OCCASIONALLY PELLETS IN HOPPER AT ALL TIMES MEAT EATERS NOT FED ON SUNDAY

Again, the passage of time has dulled my memory, but special mention must go not only to Dennis but also to John Buchan, Irene Blues, Denise Dempster, Harvey Smith and June McQueen who were present when I worked at the Zoo in those first years.

When my parents took the occasional holiday or were visiting other zoos, this posed a problem. Although I thought I was responsible enough to be left on my own, this was not desirable if any animals made a bid for freedom or there was bad weather. As you can imagine it was not like asking your son or daughter to look after the family pet when you went off for a couple of weeks. You were looking after a zoo full of animals, some of which were dangerous or just wanted to explore the wider world. On these occasions John Buchan would come to stay at the house.

As well as his companionship, he also introduced me to a variety of musical tastes when we had the occasional party. I still like Bob Dylan to this day.

Above all, and I don't know if it is my selective memory, I cannot remember many days at the Zoo in those early years when there wasn't a lot of fun. Maybe they were just simpler times, still with pressures, but not the deluge which the younger folk

John Buchan and Humphrey at one of the many tea parties

54

seem to be experiencing today.

The staff were extremely devoted to the animals in their care. You only have to look at the articles in the press to see the hurt in John Buchan's eyes when the deaths of Humphrey and Heather, the chimps, were reported. Apart from the initial time when Humphrey was donated to the Zoo and was kept in our house, John looked after the chimp and when Heather arrived John was in sole charge of them. He stayed with them if they were showing any signs of stress or minor ailments; they were at that time his bairns. When the financial lifeline to the Zoo was rejected by the Council, John had the unenviable task of putting Humphrey and Heather into crates for their transportation to Chester Zoo. John accompanied them and was complimented on the good health of both chimps which seems to fly in the face of a comment attributed to Councillor John Sewel who stated, *'It is known from their health history that Humphrey was not a well chimp'*. John spent a week with them to help them settle in. You can only imagine his hurt when both chimps succumbed to a virus to which they seemed to have no will to resist.

'Humphrey and Heather lost will to live because of zoo switch'

Former keeper accuses after two chimps die

In another example of dedication, Denise Dempster, who was to become John Buchan's wife, noticed that Leyla a newly acquired lioness from a safari park in England was fretting. Denise did not hesitate to take the lioness home to Bucksburn. Now the growling from the bedroom which greeted Denise's mother did give her a bit of a scare, not to mention the fact that the milkman nearly dropped the milk bottles when Denise took the young lioness out for a walk first thing in the morning.

I am really sorry that I cannot give all the staff a name check, but a lack of records in the minutes of the Society's meetings has made this impossible. I have however, listed some below, and I hope those missing from the list will understand.

Keepers

Dennis Milne	First Head Keeper
John Buchan	Head Keeper after Dennis left
Irene Blues	
Leslie Carnie	
Denise Dempster	
James Forrest	
Stuart Kemp	
John Laing	
Hazel Lindsay	
June McQueen	
Derek Morgan	
Iain Morrice	
James Rothnie	
Ray Slaven	
Harvey Smith	
Valerie Turner	
Mrs Wainwright	
Jim Cook (Part-time)	

Additional Staff

Walter Fowler	Deputy Manager
Mrs Womersley	Cleaner
Mr Womersley (Part-time)	Handyman
Jimmy Ross (Part-time)	Gardener and Handyman

Keeper John Laing (1971) with Lass, the Wolf

Harvey Smith with Larry, St Kilda Sheep (1967) & Irene Blues with Humbolt's Woolly Monkey

Volunteers

As most organisations know, the contribution made by volunteers is important. Indeed, many charities could not function without its volunteer workforce. From the time the Zoo was a mere concept, volunteers were the backbone of the Society. From 1961 until the Zoo was a physical entity in 1966 no one was paid for the work undertaken. This included all the Management meetings, the distribution of donated animals, the running of various events within the Senior and Junior Zoo Clubs, the setting up and manning of the stands at shows, and both housing and feeding of the animals in their temporary accommodation.

Between my memory and the notes left by my father there is insufficient detail to list or acknowledge all the individuals; the boys and girls and men and women know who they are. Hopefully they will look back on those days as volunteers with fond memories.

As you can imagine, most young boys and girls arrived to help with perhaps a rose-tinted view of the role they were to play. They soon realised that the reality was less glamorous. They soon knew how to wield a fork, spade and bucket or wheelbarrow to muck out everything from donkeys to dingoes and everything else in between!

All this youthful enthusiasm had to be controlled, as the signage in the Zoo said, 'They Bite'. This applied to most things; even cuddly-looking kinkajous were not short in mounting a team assault if something was causing their displeasure. It was always my ambition to be able to count to 10 on my fingers at the end of each day. That is not to say that I didn't get bitten, just not seriously.

I have detailed in another section the near fatal incident that befell a young lad at the paws of the pumas, but I also remember the occasion when an enthusiastic helper decided to take it upon herself to clean not only the outside of the glass in the gibbon enclosure, but also the inside. In my experience apes and primates love attention and being stroked, tickled and scratched, but they would soon let you know when they were bored. You just knew from their demeanour or body language if they were having an off day and you were not welcome in their space. So it was with Monk, the male gibbon, on this particular day. The girl was busily cleaning the inside of the glass. Unfortunately, it was not up to Monk's standards, and he inflicted a serious bite to her thigh. The girl was retrieved from the enclosure, and I assume she was taken to hospital for a check-up and the obligatory tetanus injection. This, depending on the member of nursing staff administering it, could be as sore as the original injury. Thankfully, I cannot remember any serious injuries to any of the volunteers being recorded at the Zoo, though there were a few close calls with the red deer and the pumas. It would be easy to attribute this to good luck, but it is testament to the professionalism of the full-time staff who understood the risks and ensured that many of these bright-eyed and enthusiastic young things went home safely at the end of the day. They might have been exhausted and covered in muck, but they usually returned the next day with fresh clothes and boundless enthusiasm.

One of the unexpected perks of working or volunteering at the Zoo in those early years was the arrangement made with Hazlehead Restaurant. Mrs Glass, the Manager, had agreed to a reduced cost for all Zoo personnel. Goodness knows how many plates of pie, beans and chips were consumed over the years that the Zoo was in existence.

Education

Education was at the heart of the Zoo's ethos, perhaps not surprising given the founding fathers were predominantly academics.

One of the first education meetings, held on Monday 19th February 1962, saw an attendance of 75 head teachers and principal teachers of science from the schools within the City. They were there to hear how the Society intended to assist with educational programmes through visits to Edinburgh Zoo, lectures and film shows.

In 1964 Lil de Kock wrote to the Director of Education, Aberdeenshire Council, highlighting various initiatives where the Zoo and the schools could cooperate: from schools adopting individual animals, drawing and painting competitions, and an inter-school quiz. Other proposals were more related to the educational aspects of loaning small animals to classes or individual pupils during the winter. There was the possibility of loans of animals for specific projects, assistance with more advanced studies in animal behaviour, demonstrations and displays for teaching. Exhibits other than animals, monthly reports on events and developments, assistance on specific tasks and the offer of assistance with art and photography projects were all suggested.

There was no lack of enthusiasm for the Zoo from the youngsters in Aberdeen with 32,000 children attending the Zoo within the first five weeks of it opening.

In the early years the Society identified the need to keep the public, in particular children, informed. A Quarterly Zoo News was issued giving a candid report on the progress of the Zoo and animals. It was not sugar coated and full of spin, but gave an honest update on new arrivals, deaths of animals and the main issues which were having an effect on the Zoo.

A variety of activities was employed from crosswords and join the dots to picnics at the Muir of Dinnet, and an annual trip to Edinburgh Zoo. The word was spread with talks to the Scout Association and the Society facilitated talks from Armand Denis. With televisions becoming more accessible, even if only in black and white, many will remember him, as along with his wife Michaela, they brought wildlife into our living rooms. Picnics and outings were also organised with the Senior Zoo Club to places such as Skatie Shore, just north of Stonehaven.

In the minutes of the AGM held on 27th May 1964, a report was given for the year, which detailed the Lord Provost presenting prizes for Nature Week, a Nature Treasure Hunt, a visit to Torry Marine Laboratory, nature films including one at the Odeon Cinema, and a demonstration of how to look after an aquarium. A further two excursions were noted, one to Culterty Field Station and Forvie National Nature Reserve, and an outing to Craibstone College of Agriculture. It is evident that the Society was committed to bringing the natural world to the children of Aberdeen and the children appreciated it. The attendance at the monthly meetings averaged about 250. This is an outstanding figure of which many a club in Aberdeen today would be extremely envious.

Notes from the Junior Zoo Committee highlighted the variety of activities included in the proposed programme and demonstrated the commitment of the Committee to the Zoo as an educational resource.

The list included: -

a) Summer Photographic Competitions Under 12s and Over 12s
b) Visit   Fowlsheugh Bird Sanctuary by boat (over 12s only)
c) Programme   Meet the animals
                       Game Parks
                       Inter-school Quiz
d) Film show   Under the Southern Cross (Armand & Michaela Denis)
e) Zoo Picnics   Bennachie and Muir of Dinnet
f) Film Show   Between the Tides
g) Zoo Picnic   Collieston
h) Visit   Safari Park near Stirling (1970)
i) Day Trip   Dundee Zoo
j) Film Show   The Coral Reef
                       The Water Spider
                       The Octopus
                       The Awakening (Brown Bear Cubs)

To supplement these activities the Zoo issued three educational pamphlets on keeping stick insects, mice and hamsters.

It was not just the children who were educated; the Senior Zoo Club held talks each month in the Senior Common Room at Marischal College.

Films were a great source of information and for example 'Wild Highlands', a British Transport Film, was screened.

Talks covered a wide range of subject matter such as a lecture by Inspector Taylor of the Aberdeen Association for the Prevention of Cruelty to Animals, a travelogue of Kathmandu, Californian National Parks, Grouse, Birds of the North East of Scotland and one with the intriguing title, Noises Fish Make.

In 1966 it was very clear that the Society was committed to the ethos of making the Zoo an educational centre for the whole of the North East of Scotland. By way of an example at a special meeting, convened on 15th September 1966, to accept Geoff Stevens's resignation and offer my father the post of Zoo Manager, the subject of salaries and future plans was aired. There was a discussion regarding the appointment of an Educational Organiser to arrange programmes in the Zoo for school children during the winter months. A starting salary of £1,350 to £1,500 per annum was provisionally suggested, compared to the £800 plus accommodation paid to my father as Manager of the Zoo. It is also interesting to note the aspirations of the Society who recognised that if the Zoo increased in size a Zoo Director may be appointed, a post which would have been senior to those of the Zoo Manager and the Educational Organiser.

Later that year, the Society decided to appoint a Zoo Biologist, and Gayle Freyer took up the post in January 1967. Unfortunately, Gayle resigned in May that year due to a protracted period of ill health. It was decided to re-evaluate the position once the Zoo was more established.

The Zoo's educational achievements were recognised beyond the North East of Scotland as my father was invited to present a paper at a conference on 'Education in Zoos' in Amsterdam in August 1968. Aberdeen Zoo was one of only 20 of the 289 zoos in Europe invited to attend.

I have transcribed below my father's presentation entitled 'Children at Work' as summarised by the organisers to demonstrate the initiatives which the Zoo had put in place to help engage and educate the young visitors.

Children at Work

Aberdeen Zoo has been open only a few years. Various methods are used to interest children in the Zoo and in animals.

- *Schools are encouraged to 'adopt' Zoo animals. At the school's request, information is sent about an animal, and the cost of its feeding, e.g. children of one school pay one penny each per week towards the upkeep of a pair of seals. This amounts to £1-£2 per week for the Zoo. Some schools come to visit the animals they adopt, or Mr Leslie goes to the school and gives a talk. In order to ensure success, it is necessary to have the interest of the Headmaster of the school, or a biology teacher.*
- *Schools raise funds to buy new animals. With the help of the press one school decided to raise £1,000 towards buying a small elephant.*
- *Weekly articles on animals in the Saturday edition of a daily newspaper.*
- *Junior Zoo Club activities. Fee - ten shillings per annum. There are 600-700 junior members. Juniors have free access to the Zoo, may assist keepers, have film shows, nature trails, animal picnic. Juniors interview visitors on: animals best liked, animals they miss (elephant!), effectiveness of paid publicity.*
- *Zoo Guide Group (juniors of 12-18 years old) meets on a Saturday morning once a month. They have a two-hour talk on one particular animal or group of animals. After this they take an oral examination, which entitles them to a Junior Guide Badge. They may then offer information to the general public. In groups of 10-12 they are to be given 'insect boxes' to furnish themselves, collect material, etc., also fish. They do all the work themselves. At the end of the term prizes are allotted.*
- *School projects (for winter season): schools are encouraged to design Zoo posters; one school is supplying animal photographs for the Zoo notice boards; one school is making a scale model of the Zoo.*
- *Assistance from junior members: 11-18 year olds may help keepers (1 or 2 children to one keeper), after they have first been 'tried out' sweeping paths and emptying wastepaper bins. 'Senior helpers', 15-18 years old, give pony and donkey rides. Junior members assist the keepers in patrolling the Zoo during the summer evenings.*

Discussion

The use of tame animals was discussed, especially for small children. Opposite tendencies are noted. In Seattle the Zoo participates in displays in stores, where people may handle the animals, to know what they feel like. Others argue for displaying an animal in its natural surroundings as the wild animal it is, not to be touched.

The best solution seemed to be to have a separate 'small children Zoo' a department of the Zoo with especially tame animals that can be handled and do not belong to the normal collection.

I believe the initiatives introduced by the Zoo and presented at the conference clearly demonstrate the Zoo's commitment to education. All of these initiatives incurred a cost in the form of wages and material resources to keep the young people engaged, which had to be carried by the Zoo. As illustrated during the presentation, the following schools were involved at the early stages of the animal adoption scheme: Walker Dam School – grey seals, Fernielea School - wallaby, Bridge of Don School – red deer and Boddam School – gibbon.

And all of this from a Zoo which had only been opened to the public for three years.

The Zoo continued to provide a much-needed educational resource to the pupils in the North East and in 1969 the Zoo hosted 71 school parties comprising 2,401 pupils and 518 adults from all over Aberdeenshire.

Throughout the next few years the Zoo continued to host visits from school pupils and to educate children either through talks or with educational signage.

Pupils from Walker Dam School meeting Thorfinn their adopted new baby seal, only the second zoo-born seal in the whole of Europe

Pupils from Newhills School with their adopted fox, Promise

Pupils from Inverallochy School, Fraserburgh visiting the grey seals

Elephant Fund

WE WANT A JUMBO: Morag, Fiona and Graham Fyfe and Fiona Ross have a novel idea to raise money to buy an elephant for the zoo. The children raised £20.

Fundraising for the Elephant Fund (1969)

For many in Aberdeen and the North East of Scotland who remember the Zoo, one of their main memories will be of the Elephant Fund.

This initiative initially enthused many across the region, and then contributed to some adverse publicity and disappointment when the promised elephant did not materialise. The fund was then used to buy three lions.

The Elephant Fund was started by Aberdeen Journals, following a poll in the paper to determine which animal the public wished to see most at the Zoo. The result suggested that they would like to see one of the world's most iconic species here in Aberdeen.

I have to say at this point that my father was not in favour of getting an elephant, partly because of the area of land required to house one. As you will note from the other sections on the location and demise of the Zoo, the expansion plans for the Zoo had always been a bone of contention.

As well as the physical area involved, the cost of purchasing the elephant, and its food bill, there is the cost of a dedicated keeper. Elephants are gregarious creatures and require one-to-one attention. The late 1960s were different times, and the discussions around the recruitment of an elephant keeper included the following: *'First of all a keeper is needed - preferably a country lad who could grow up alongside a baby elephant, for the life span of man and elephant are pretty similar'.*

Despite the doubts of the Society, Aberdeen Journals insisted that it would be good publicity and launched the appeal, saying it would take months if not years to raise the required £1,500. Not for the first time the generosity of the people of the North East had been underestimated. It took only 10 weeks to raise £1,000, the original target of the appeal.

The effort was spurred on by headlines such as: -

Aberdeen Zoo could have an elephant if they could raise £1,000

Pupils Jumbo sized bid for elephant

In the Running for a Jumbo

Offering goes for a Jumbo

IN THE RUNNING FOR A JUMBO

● Running themselves into the ground—that's the pupils of Inchgarth School as they make an all-out effort to get fit for their campaign.

The pupils seem determined that Aberdeen Zoo will have an elephant.

IT'S YEG WALK tomorrow — and all systems go for Inchgarth School's bid to get Aberdeen Zoo an elephant.

Inchgarth pupils, the first group to rally to the "Evening Express" call for £1000 to buy an elephant, are in the running to make another big donation.

And literally RUNNING to be in the running!

For Inchgarth's 100-strong Young Elephant Group have been jog-trotting all week to get fit for the 14-mile sponsored YEG walk.

According to member of staff Mr Robert Houston, his biggest headache is trying to limit the numbers who want to go. Inchgarth really has taken the 'ephant idea to heart.

And since we publicised their efforts last Monday, the school's total has climbed to a jumbo-sized £15.

NEWSPAPER

It's thanks not only to the work of Inchgarth boys and girls, but to people like Mrs Ruby Cruickshank, 64 Kaimhill Circle as well. After hearing about the school's efforts through her son David, she donated £5 from selling toffee to neighbours.

ALL FOR JUMBO

By NORMAN MACPHEE

Inchgarth total is now £225

THE PUPILS of Inchgarth School have done it again. This time I have received a cheque for £75 from them—bringing their total contribution to the Aberdeen Zoo Elephant Fund to TWO HUNDRED AND TWENTY-FIVE POUNDS!

In June 1969, 150 children took part in a 14 mile walk as part of the Young Elephant Group. It was reported at the time that one pupil did not complete the course, as 10-year old John Wood almost reached the City boundary when a large dog leapt on him and bit him in the leg.

Inchgarth School was one of the first schools to get involved, and by the end of June 1969 they had collected an astounding £225.

A group in Gladstone Place raised £3/2/- (£3.10 in new money), from selling old books. The fund even benefitted from church offerings, as the Primary Sunday School at South St. Nicholas Church, Kincorth, donated one guinea.

By July 1969 the headlines read 'The Elephant Fund is Growing Fast – Our elephant is about halfway to the Zoo' – the fund totalled £823.

Funds were being raised from an assortment of jumble sales, penny fairs and 'guess the number of sweets in a jar'.

One of the most unusual donations was reported in the press. A Miss Elizabeth Walker found a purse containing £50, a considerable amount at the time. She believed the Postal Order for 2/6, (12.5 new pence) was a derisory amount of money as a reward for her honesty, and donated all of it to the Elephant Fund.

By the end of July 1969, the Elephant Fund was closed having raised £1,245/10/00.

By July 1970 the Elephant Fund was causing embarrassment to Aberdeen Journals and the Zoo. A meeting was called to discuss the fund.

At a Special Meeting convened on 1st July 1970, Basil Parrish, the Society's Convener, outlined the reasons for the meeting namely: -

1. that the possession of the Elephant Fund money was causing Mr MacPhee of Aberdeen Journals some embarrassment, as children and parents were beginning to ask questions.

2. that accordingly Mr MacPhee, at a Society meeting, indicated his intention of pressuring the Society into buying an elephant now. The elephant was to be housed on the present Zoo site, in the knowledge that no further

ground will be available for at least two years (as stated in a letter from Aberdeen City Council).

3. that some action must be taken to save the good name of the Society in the eyes of the public.

The Society had managed to source an elephant from Birmingham. A two and half-year old female Indian elephant was available at a cost of £1,350. In addition, the Society had looked at the ramifications of fitting the elephant in the existing confines of the Zoo. This would mean sacrificing the duck area and using the existing duck pond for the elephant. The cost of all these alterations was estimated, together with the cost of feeding the elephant and the additional keeper resource required. The decision was taken to buy the elephant subject to finalising all the costs.

This decision was conveyed to Norman McPhee. At the Society meeting held on 17th July 1970, there was a resumé of the decision taken at the Special Meeting and it was reported that Norman McPhee had undertaken to make a direct approach to the Lord Provost for a donation towards the elephant enclosure once the Society agreed to the purchase.

After gleaning further information on the costs of building an enclosure, with recurring costs of a keeper and feeding the elephant, there was a protracted meeting of the Society to understand the financial implications. They even went on to discuss the health of the proposed animal. However, as it was already acclimatised, no problems were envisaged. The possibility of it breaking out meant particular attention would have to be paid to its security. Regarding exercise, *'this could be done during the evenings or when few people are about. A young animal would not be suitable for giving rides even if room in the Zoo was available'*.

After consideration of all of the above information it was decided the Zoo could buy and support an elephant.

The caveat to the above was that the Zoo needed funding from the Council to finance the alterations and building work required to house an elephant.

Approaches were made to Aberdeen City Council from both the Zoo and Aberdeen Journals and, although I am not in possession of any specific documents which track the decisions, it would appear that over the next few months there was some prevarication by Aberdeen City Council and the hopes of the Zoo getting an elephant just faded away.

It was clear that the purchase of an elephant could not be contemplated until the Zoo had more land, and only if Aberdeen City Council contributed to the cost of building a dedicated enclosure. The decision regarding the elephant was revisited by the Society on numerous occasions. They were acutely aware of the embarrassment to Aberdeen Journals, the negative publicity and the reduction in goodwill from the loyal patrons, not to mention the disappointment of so many children in the area.

In January 1972 the local press tried to keep the pressure on Aberdeen City Council by reporting that back in 1969 children had raised over £1,000 and there had been continuous negotiations for additional land to expand and to accommodate the elephant house. The land had been promised to the Zoo for the last five years, but no decision had been taken. The fund now stood at £1,346.59 with the interest accrued.

By September 1972 Links and Parks confirmed that the Zoo could not have additional land. Headlines at the time reported 'Hopes of a Bigger Zoo Fading Away'. It was therefore agreed to use the money to buy an alternative; three lion cubs. This decision was not universally welcome and in November 1972 the press featured articles with the headlines: -

Please give us our Elephant

Row Flares at Zoo over Elephant House Promise

Don't make Zoo a White Jumbo

Clear up the Jumbo Jumble

Jumbo Sized Blow for the Zoo

It's all for jumbo!

'It's a crying shame for all those children who collected'
— Mr ALLAN McKENDRICK

Row flares
at zoo over
elephant house promise

General view of Aberdeen Zoo

70

The World Wildlife Fund created
the Gavin Maxwell Otter Project
to be a memorial to Gavin Maxwell
for the study and conservation of
otters throughout the world.

The Gavin Maxwell Otter Project
in recognition of his contribution to
the furtherance of these aims
hereby bestows

The Gavin Maxwell Award

on GEORGE LESLIE

who successfully bred and maintained
in captivity *Amblonyx cinerea* at
Aberdeen Zoological Garden

On this 15th day of June 1972

Tale of the Celebrity Otter

In 1960 Gavin Maxwell published 'Ring of Bright Water' about his life in a remote location in the West of Scotland. This was a best seller and raised public awareness of the threats to the European otter. The book was used as the inspiration for a film released in 1969 starring Bill Travers and Virginia McKenna.

In 1966 Gavin Maxwell was looking for a home for two of his otters, Edal and Teko. Edal was famous as one of the stars of his books about the otters at Sandaig on the west coast of Scotland. It should be said that Gavin Maxwell was very exacting with regard to the design and siting of the enclosure.

Negotiations started with the Zoo, initially with Lil de Kock. However, things appeared to be strained at one point, and an intermediary decided to stand down, as meetings with Gavin Maxwell were 'very unpleasant'.

The discussions were then conducted between Gavin Maxwell, Basil Parrish and my father. This led to one of the most memorable weekends, not necessarily for its pleasurable nature, when the author came to stay.

He was undoubtedly a bit of a character, who was described in his biography as an aristocrat, social renegade, wartime secret agent, shark hunter, adventurer, racing driver, traveller, naturalist, poet and painter and was at the height of his fame with 'Ring of Bright Water'.

As I have alluded to earlier, my father took a drink and it was reputed that Gavin Maxwell was no stranger to a drop of whisky. The cupboard was duly stocked with four bottles of our national drink (not Irn Bru). The two bold heroes started with lots of bonhomie and I have to say that Gavin Maxwell was a very charismatic and interesting character.

I cannot remember much of the conversation, but I do remember that he had been told the date he was to die by some shaman or soothsayer in Africa. Years later my father was convinced that the prediction had come to pass.

It transpired that he could hold his drink better than my father, and in the wee small hours of the morning I was awakened by mother, who it was fair to say was in a bit a state. He and my father had had a disagreement over goodness knows what, but in their inebriated state they thought that the only way to sort this out was to have a duel. Gavin Maxwell was going to get his revolver from his car, a beautiful old Mercedes with gull-wing doors, and my father was going to get his shotgun. Thankfully, after a bit of cajoling, common sense prevailed, and the protagonists decided to go and sleep it off instead.

The World Wildlife Fund created the Gavin Maxwell Otter Project to be a memorial to Gavin Maxwell for the study and conservation of otters throughout the world.

The Gavin Maxwell Otter Project in recognition of his contribution to the furtherance of these aims hereby bestows

The Gavin Maxwell Award

on *GEORGE LESLIE*

who sucessfully bred and maintained in captivity *Amblonyx cinerea at Aberdeen Zoological Garden*

On this *15th* day of *June* 1972

J. L. Scott

Chairman World Wildlife Fund and
Gavin Maxwell Otter Project

Nicole Shelfair-Bell

Vice Chairman
Gavin Maxwell Otter Project

I recall that all four bottles had been consumed by the Sunday morning and a further two bottles were brought in an old shoe box by Basil Parrish on the Sunday. After all it would not have been the done thing for someone to clink to the door with an off-licence bag on a Sunday.

One of the abiding memories of the weekend was that Gavin Maxwell never seemed particularly drunk, whereas the same could not be said for my father who could have joined the newts in the exhibits.

On the Monday Gavin Maxwell got back into his gull-winged Mercedes Sports Coupe and sped off.

From handwritten notes it would appear that once the Zoo had constructed the enclosure it had to be inspected by a representative of Gavin Maxwell. Once approved, Edal would be transferred to the Zoo in a specially designed travelling cage. In addition, the Zoo would be responsible for all costs and the upkeep of Edal until the transfer was made. It was speculated that this transitional period could last until April 1967. Prior to the end of 1966 the Zoo obviously thought that negotiations would be successful and had Christmas cards printed featuring Edal.

After some protracted discussions about the design of the enclosure and the cost of adapting the existing area to satisfy Gavin Maxwell's specification, it is clear that the Zoo would not be home to his otters after all.

Although the Zoo failed to obtain the otters, it was quite ironic that my father was awarded the Gavin Maxwell Award a few years later when the Oriental short-clawed otters bred at Aberdeen Zoo for the first time outside Malaysia.

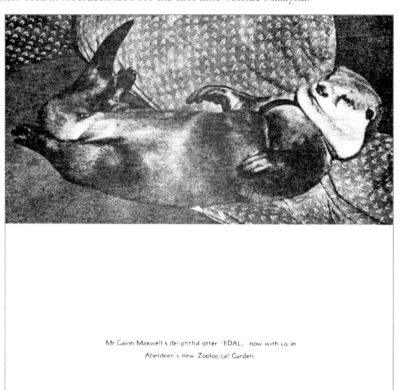

Mr Gavin Maxwell's delightful otter "EDAL," now with us in Aberdeen's new Zoological Garden

Wishing You a Happy Christmas

and a

Bright and Prosperous New Year

Edal Christmas Card

Demise of the Zoo

Four thousand back bid to save city zoo

Mr JOHN BUCHAN

THE PEOPLE of Aberdeen are staging a last-ditch fight to try to prevent the closure of Aberdeen Zoo.

During the past three weeks, almost 4000 people have signed a petition saying they are in favour of the zoo staying open.

But today Professor Bruce Salmon, chairman of the zoo management committee, said in effect, despite the future as likely the tip of the iceberg.

"I do not think that figure in any way departs the number of people who would be prepared to sign the petition if it came their way," he said today.

Zoo manager Mr John Buchan said keepers alone had collected 3300 signatures.

"The response from everyone who has signed has been one of universal sympathy," said Mr Buchan.

He said visitors to and his staff had spoken to were of the same opinion. The zoo should stay open.

He added: "People are saying the zoo is looking better now than it ever has.

"Since the closure announcement zoo attendance figures have dropped.

"Many people think the zoo has already shut," said Mr Buchan. "What they don't seem to realise is that if they don't come and see the animals now they may never see them again."

Professor Salmon said the petition will be collected this week and will be put before the meeting of the full district council on June 27.

He added: "If anyone wants to help back the zoo and add their names to the petition they can do so at the zoo itself.

"They won't have to pay entrance money — they can just sign their names at the gate.

"Last year 45,000 people visited the zoo and the previous year freely at least half were residents of Aberdeen.

"I'm sure that the vast majority would be pleased to add their names to the 4000 we already have."

But he added: "I wonder how the amount of harms that have been put out and the limited number of people attending the zoo about I think this is a very good response."

You could say that the fate of the Zoo was determined when the choice of location was made. The Society could not have known that the initial constructive collaboration between the Zoo's founding fathers and Aberdeen City Council would fall apart. I am not suggesting that there was an agenda to have the Zoo fail. Indeed, the recent refurbishment of the Pets Corner some 40 years after the demise of the Zoo would lead you to think there were some who wanted a visitor attraction in Hazlehead. However, a collaborative approach back in the 1970s may have resulted in a better outcome.

The Zoo failed for a number of reasons and through a series of circumstances. None of these would have been fatal, but collectively they conspired to ring the death knell on the Aberdeen Zoo Project.

It is well documented that the initial Zoo was to be a first phase, and that it would eventually expand to encompass a larger part of Hazlehead Park. The mature trees would be retained, and the enclosures would be sculpted sympathetically to enhance rather than detract from the amenity of the Park.

The early enthusiasm displayed by Aberdeen City Council's elected officials and officers changed and their successors generally were less enthusiastic about the Zoo. It is evident from the Society's minutes of meetings that the area adjacent to the Zoo containing the potting sheds and used by Links and Parks became a pawn in a bigger game. From the minutes and the original discussions and agreements this area was eventually to be given over to the Zoo. In 1967 the planning department of Aberdeen City Council favoured expansion into Hazlehead Park. Despite this recommendation, in May 1967 the Society was advised that the potting sheds would not be available for some considerable time.

By August 1967 David Welch opposed the expansion of the Zoo at Hazlehead. It was then suggested that a 100-acre site to the south of Aberdeen would make a good location. Although this is not specifically mentioned by name, I think it is safe to assume that this is the site of Doonies Farm at Nigg. The Society deemed this to be too costly having effectively invested so much time, effort and money into Hazlehead.

As a result of this refusal to move, David Welch advised the Society that he still opposed the plans for expansion at Hazlehead, and intimated that it would be at least 18 to 24 months before the potting shed area could be made available.

This undoubtedly put pressure on the Zoo, as although the original plan was to have animals that were indigenous to Scotland, the public wanted to see the more exotic species. As you have seen in the section on the Elephant Fund, this refusal to allow the use of the area of the potting sheds had severe ramifications for many people.

It would be easy to think that there was a conspiracy against the Zoo, and you could forgive the Society for being perplexed at the mixed messages they were receiving from Aberdeen City Council.

In April 1968 Links and Parks, in a positive move, offered to replant the whole of the free flight aviary free of charge. In August of that year Aberdeen City Council intimated to the Society that a delegation, including the Lord Provost and David Welch, were to visit Hazlehead Park. The purpose of this visit was to look at the old Head Gardener's Cottage at the entrance to the park, with a view to making it available to the Zoo. As you will see later on in the chapter entitled 'How do you Measure Success', this area could have been used for an isolation and hospital unit, which would have allowed the Zoo to apply for membership of the Federation of Zoological Gardens of Great Britain and Ireland.

However, four months later Aberdeen City Council announced it had decided to refurbish the Head Gardener's Cottage and use it as a small shop which would stock items in direct competition to the Zoo.

In another demonstration of the shifting priorities, in September 1969 it was reported that the potting shed area would not be made available to the Zoo for at least three years.

In addition to the pressure being applied due to the lack of space for expansion, funding was becoming an issue as reported in March 1970, where it was noted that a sixth of the income was going on rent and rates to Aberdeen City Council.

As time went on further pressure was applied by Aberdeen City Council as they queried the direction of the Zoo. Meetings were held with representatives from Aberdeen City Council and were noted in the Society's minutes as 'profitless'.

All the above conspired to frustrate the Society, the majority of whom, it must be remembered, had day jobs, and were not being recompensed for their time in managing the Zoo. The Zoo continued, albeit living from hand to mouth.

In an apparent U-turn in November 1973, Aberdeen City Council declared that the potting shed area could be made available if the Zoo put it to an 'acceptable use' to them. In what must have seemed an insult, as part of this agreement the Zoo was being asked to give its larger animals to Aberdeen City Council to help establish a Country Park. In an even more curious development, it was suggested that small animal exhibits could be established at caravan sites and parks around the City. Looking at the minutes and notes one can only think that the Society was completely perplexed and confused by the mercurial proposals being put forward by Aberdeen City Council.

Roll forward five months, and Aberdeen City Council wrote to the Zoo suggesting that they might 'farm out' some of the animals and asking for a sketch map of a re-planned Zoo to cut down on the 'noise and smell'.

The saga of the potting sheds continued and in February 1975 Aberdeen City Council offered this area to the Zoo on the condition that it was turned into a play area and not for animal enclosures!

In 1976 Aberdeen City Council was continuing to pressurise the Zoo into only exhibiting small indigenous animals and by April that year it wanted the Zoo established elsewhere.

I think it is worth stating that I left school in 1969. Although a career with animals might have seemed the obvious choice, I really felt that I could not work constantly with my father. I suppose, when your life has been dictated to by animals, you rebel. I therefore entered the construction industry. I still helped some evenings and weekends at the Zoo until I married in 1973 and moved away from the Zoo. I still maintained an active interest in nature and the environment and consider that interest, and in particular birdwatching, has enriched my life considerably.

From 1969 to 1977 when I was not directly involved in the Zoo, I did not realise the pressures being exerted on the Zoo from all sides. Possibly the main one was the financial pressures on an enterprise which relied heavily on seasonal activity, and which could not cut costs when the visitors didn't brave the weather; animals still had to be fed and cared for. The Zoo put pressure on itself by continuing the quest to educate and inform the public and in response the public wanted to see more exotic animals. You can make up your own mind with regard to pressures exerted by Aberdeen City Council, but I have tried to show their change of attitude.

Referring to the articles in the local press at the time, I cannot get over how the war of words was fought so publicly in the papers. The public was very supportive during this spat. Typical of this was a letter received which stated that the closure of the Zoo would be *'a great loss to the city and a blow to what is becoming an increasingly important area of nature conservation'*.

This is particularly relevant when you look at the breeding success at the Zoo. Some of the animals born were not rare or in danger of extinction, but it is interesting that almost 50 years later there are proposals to reintroduce captive bred wildcats to bolster the wild population. Wildcats were one of the species successfully bred at the Zoo.

Although there was general support for the Zoo Project from within Aberdeen City Council, there were times when councillors let their personal feelings on zoos be known. In another public attack on the Zoo, Councillor Frank Magee voiced his opposition to the Zoo and was reported as having said *'I hate zoos, I absolutely hate them. You find that most zoos house shabby tigers with apes standing outside to look at them'*. He claimed that there was an *'appalling mess'* at Hazlehead and conditions were disgraceful. *'I could not take my grandchildren along there'*. As a result of his stance Councillor Frank Magee had been 'attacked' by a member of the public who was presumably in favour of the Zoo.

The public were still very supportive of the Zoo, even though it was effectively in its death throes. On the eve of an Aberdeen City Council meeting convened to hear the recommendations of a Special Committee on the future of the Zoo, 10,000 members of the public took advantage of an open day at the Zoo.

As you will see later in this section the Zoo asked whether Aberdeen City Council could provide £10,000 to assist with much needed maintenance and renovations. In the end Aberdeen City Council voted against providing funds for the Zoo by a 31 to 10 majority.

The war of words between the Zoo and Aberdeen City Council was played out very publicly in the local press, with accusations and counter accusations flying back and forth. To highlight the degree of animosity the following headlines have been included with a brief narrative of the articles to demonstrate the strength of feeling from both sides.

Where does the Zoo go from here?

Where does the zoo go from here?

LEFT: Looking through the wire mesh of his pen is Aberdeen Zoo's 10-month-old lion cub MacNicol, reared from the age of three weeks by zoo manager George Leslie in his own home.

RIGHT: This scene at the zoo is not as dangerous as it may look as, after an inquiry about safety measures by "The Press and Journal," the zoo authorities have mounted a perspex shield in front of the mesh.

This headline from an article by Andrew Maywood was followed by a fairly good summary of the situation in which the Zoo found itself. The accusations of 'over-crowded, dirty, noisy and smelly' had been levied at the Zoo by Aberdeen City Council. Bob Ralph had responded by saying that if the Council had given the additional land, some of these accusations could be dealt with. It is interesting that Dr Ralph also said that only one letter of complaint had been received by the Zoo.

It is fair to say that there had been the odd complaint over the years. In September 1971 Allan McKendrick, the solicitor and legal adviser to the Zoo, wrote an open letter to Aberdeen Journals. This set the record straight about various aspects of the Zoo. Firstly, he commented on the obvious health of the animals in the Zoo, presumably to counter some comment regarding the untidiness of the cages. He pointed out that with over 3,000 visitors a day in summer it was difficult to clear half-eaten carcasses from the lion and wolf enclosures. He went on to confirm that the Zoo is run by an independent society limited by guarantee which has no connection with Aberdeen City Council. Allan also went on to say that the Zoo paid Aberdeen City Council an annual rent for the site and received no financial assistance, unlike zoos such as Edinburgh and London.

In the Andrew Maywood article, it was pointed out that the crux of the problem was the additional land. Bob Ralph again pointed out that the Zoo had been promised additional land even before the Zoo opened, a fact verified by the minutes of the original meetings. By now it was clear that there was a limited amount of support for the Zoo within Aberdeen City Council, with only Councillor Alexander Mutch being supportive. The article again highlighted that Aberdeen City Council wanted the Zoo to move to a site possibly at Doonies Farm near the Bay of Nigg, but equally there was no support, financial or otherwise, to assist the Zoo with such a move. It is well worth remembering that back in the 60s and 70s Hazlehead was served by a bus route, whereas Doonies Farm had limited public transport.

In defence of what seems to be ill-informed statements from various Aberdeen City Council officials, Bob Ralph highlighted the numerous breeding successes including grey seals and the Oriental short-clawed otters.

This article, together with others, demonstrated that Aberdeen City Council had a change of heart from the original discussions in the mid-1960s when there was wide support for the Zoo Project.

Animals in Zoo 'are too big'

In May 1976 Lord Provost Robert Lennox blamed the introduction of larger animals in the Zoo for the accusations of over-crowding and smell. He also confirmed that any expansion at Hazlehead would be against the policy of Aberdeen City Council. The Lord Provost was quoted as saying '*the Zoo was originally built by Aberdeen City Council as a small zoo for children, but too large animals have been introduced and now it needs expanding, which we are reluctant to allow. It was never intended to be the kind of size that would lead to expansion at Hazlehead Park*'.

I would comment that the Lord Provost should have been better briefed, as it is clear from all the records of the original discussions, before the Zoo became a physical reality, that the site occupied was the first phase of 2 acres and the second phase was to be an additional 10 acres. In addition, Aberdeen City Council may have commissioned the building of the Zoo, but they had no input or responsibility when it came to either the policy or the management of the Zoo.

Hard bargaining over the future of Aberdeen Zoo

In the present economic climate a questionmark hangs over Hazlehead

Hard bargaining over the future of Aberdeen Zoo

(LEFT) HUMPHREY the chimp shares a pie with head keeper John Buchan. Kingswells Caravan Site.

(RIGHT) VICTORIA the lioness seems to be pondering how long she may be allowed to live in her present surroundings.

In September 1976 my father was quoted as saying he was bitter at Aberdeen City Council's continued lack of cooperation since the early days of the zoo. *'In everything with the town over the past 10 years we have got nowhere. They have promised us the Kingdom of Heaven and nothing has been forthcoming. It appears to me, because of lack of support that they would like to see the Society going bankrupt'.*

City zoo animals face slaughter

In what was described as a frank interview my father set out succinctly the problems which faced the Zoo. The constraints imposed due to the lack of support by Aberdeen City Council had adversely affected the Zoo and they were now faced with a decision whether to sell animals or pay off keepers. It is evident that if the number of keepers were reduced, this would affect the quality of care. This would lead to a downward spiral which would ultimately result in the reduction of the viability of the Zoo, and an end of an attractive destination for the local population and visitors to the city.

It is also worthy of note that Dr Ralph had announced his intention to resign stating *'I am really just fed up with the problems of running the Zoo and the unreasonableness of Aberdeen City Council in the past'.*

Snakes alive – a protest

A petition with over 6,000 signatures collected over a week was handed to Aberdeen City Council by Dr Ralph and John Buchan; the snake part was the boa constrictor used as a bit of animal interest.

John Buchan and boa constrictors

Reducing the size of animals at the Zoo

It is clear that Aberdeen City Council had nothing against zoos as such. They advocated moving to a site beside the Bay of Nigg. However, it seems that Aberdeen City Council was against anything which would result in an expansion at Hazlehead, which was the original proposal back in the embryonic days of the Zoo.

Headlines such as 'Leisure Chief: Think small and save the Zoo' and 'Zoo to go Native. Exotic species will be sold in scaling down scheme'. David Welch is quoted as saying some animals were not particularly attractive at all times of the year especially when shedding their coats. This attitude resonates with me, as my father commented that there were some zoos in Britain which regularly purchased bear cubs only to put them down when they were too big and unmanageable. Surely no one would condone this or similar practices merely to have the animals more appealing to the general public all year round.

Defending the Accusations

Accusations were made by Councillor John Sewel, the leader of Aberdeen City Council's Labour Group, regarding financial mismanagement. The Zoo was looking for support of £10,000 to carry out essential maintenance work. However, Councillor Sewel reported that the Zoo needed £160,000. I have always believed that the truth lies somewhere between the two amounts. The chasm between these two figures makes it difficult to decide where the true amount lies. In response to these accusations, Harry Morrice, the Treasurer to the Zoo, defended the financial position stating '*the Zoo has not been mismanaged financially*'. I obviously do not have detailed knowledge of the financial situation and whose figures are the more accurate, but when the Zoo was wound up and all debts had been paid, there was a tiny surplus which was donated to the World Wildlife Fund. Councillor Sewel added '*their finances were in such a mess that they were likely to go bankrupt this summer and might have to cease their activities*'. These accusations regarding the finances were vehemently denied by Harry Morrice.

In another public attack on the Zoo, the health of the animals was called into question. The Zoo vet, Hugh Kay, challenged the claims made by Councillor Frank Magee in an BBC TV interview in which he had allegedly stated that the animals were '*emaciated*'. Hugh came out fighting saying '*it is demonstrable nonsense to say that any of the animals in Aberdeen Zoo are emaciated – a brief visit could make this clear to anyone*'.

Additionally, my father defended the health of the animals citing the regular attendance of SSPCA officers to provide an independent check on the health and care of the animals.

Possibly in an effort to justify Aberdeen City Council's decisions, Councillor John Sewel was quoted as saying that in addition to the financial mismanagement the trouble with the Zoo arose from the Society's *unwise stocking policy*.

With regard to the 'unwise stocking policy' it is evident that the Councillors and officials who had been instrumental at the start of the Zoo Project were no longer in post and over the years the original enthusiastic backing was no longer there.

Dissenting Voices in the Council

The decision not to give a lifeline to the Zoo was not unanimous. Councillor Bernard Morrison accused the subcommittee of scaring the public with the £160,000 which was said the Zoo needed to bring it up to standard. Another headline of the time was 'Roar of Protest in Fight to Save Zoo' and the article went on to accuse a group of Councillors of misleading the public to get rid of the City's Zoo.

Disposal of Animals

When it became apparent that there was no alternative but to close the Zoo, a list of surplus animals was drawn up.

This was with a view to finding homes for:

3 Lions

3 Wolves

2 Bears

6 Dingoes

15 Monkeys

5 Llamas

1 Alligator

2 Pumas

Various deer

Collection of Snakes

Finances – A Perennial Problem

It could be said that the Zoo survived by sailing close to the wind, but the reality was that the Zoo made a surplus each year apart from 1973 when it made a loss of

£2,641. Despite Aberdeen City Council agreeing at the outset to support the Zoo to the tune of £1,000 each year, it was never asked to contribute towards the running costs and charged the Zoo an economic rent.

There is further irony to the financial situation when, in a letter to Ian Maclure (Depute Director of Law and Administration) dated 22nd October 1975, Dr Ralph stated *'it is obvious that there is some hardening opposition from the Town towards the Zoo in its present form, and the Society cannot satisfactorily continue with such a bad relationship'*. It would appear that as a result of this letter the Leisure, Recreation and Tourism Committee provided £2,000 to support the Zoo and a further £2,000 was given by the Education Committee.

Finding a Common Ground

Roll forward three months and Prof. Eric Salzen wrote to David Welch enclosing a list of animals and asking him to mark up the animals which were deemed unsuitable for a Zoo receiving support from Aberdeen City Council. Prof. Salzen highlighted that if they wanted immediate action many animals would have to be killed.

It is evident from the minutes of meetings that the Society were trying to find common ground with Aberdeen City Council as recorded in the following:

10/3/76 – Minutes of Meeting between representatives of City of Aberdeen District Council and representatives of Aberdeen and North of Scotland Zoological Society

Councillor Sewel – Chairman   *Mr Parrish – President*

Councillor Christie   *Prof. Salzen - VP*

                                                      Dr Ralph – Secretary

                                                      Mr Morrice – Treasurer

The meeting had under consideration a document which purports to set out the general policy of the Society in managing the Zoo and lists the present stock in the Zoo.

On the question of large non-indigenous animals – Mr Parrish stated that certain exotic non-indigenous species had been in the Zoo from the start and that the Society had had the impression that the Council's predecessors had not objected to this.

Prof. Salzen pointed out that the Zoo was having to make do with the limited space available and the Society urgently required additional ground to the south to extend the Zoo and improve conditions for the public and the animals.

Prof. Salzen confirmed that the Society would be prepared, for the purposes of clarification, to state categorically in such policy statement that the major purpose and objective of the Zoo was the exhibition of small indigenous animals.

Councillor Sewel stated that in the meantime the Council's representatives would not be prepared to recommend that the Council give a firm commitment to continuing financial support.

At the end of 1976 a document was tabled, author unknown, which rather succinctly details the problems encountered by the Zoo:

Points for consideration – December 1976.

a) Comment on permanent shortage of funds.

b) Present shortage of funds.

c) General shortage of funds – General depressing effect on management.

d) Relevant Factors – Number of paid admissions have been dropping considerably in last few years – experienced by most zoos.

e) Conclusion – The history of cash shortage, allied to the present economic climate of the country, makes any 'easy' solutions impossible. The morale of the present management committee is low.

The City of Aberdeen District Council might be interested in helping if all the large and exotic animals are removed, leaving only a Children's Corner. The purpose of the Society would in these circumstances cease to be fulfilled.

My father took all these things to heart as he knew that the demise of the Zoo would result in animals being put down or sold. Indeed, one of the approaches received to purchase some animals was someone acting on behalf of a taxidermist. Due to these pressures my father took solace in alcohol. As he realised the impact on the Zoo, and particularly on the livestock because of the impasse with Aberdeen City Council, he took to the bottle with a vengeance. As a result, my father was asked to resign which he did do with effect from 31st December 1976 as recorded in the minutes

AXE TO FALL ON ABERDEEN ZOO IN AUGUST

QUOTE

"The council cannot possibly afford to meet the estimated £130,000 to £160,000 needed for short-term improvements to the zoo."—COUNCILLOR JOHN SEWEL

Please save our zoo

SOME of the most touching letters we have received expressing views about the threatened closure of Aberdeen Zoo have come from a class of seven-year-olds.

Pamela Cummings and Aileen Russell, both pupils in class 3R2 at Dyce Primary School, delivered 14 letters to the "Evening Express" written by their classmates.

Pamela, of 11 Glendholme Court, Dyce, took a newspaper cutting about the zoo to school and the teacher suggested they write to us.

Mrs Linda Keith, their class teacher, said: "When Pamela's mother sent her along with the cutting asking for the public's views, we had a discussion about why the zoo would be closing down and what would be happening to the animals. The children were all rather upset so I thought it would be nice if they wrote a letter to the paper.

"Their last teacher took them to the zoo, so the fact that they had seen the animals, and they all had a favourite, brought the situation home to them."

Here are some of the extracts from the letters:

"How would you like to be killed and the little baby will not have eney thing to look forward to eksept being killed."—Karen Milne.

"I think it will be sad for the children. Woulld you like it if you were an anamall. And I will miss the grila."—John Scott.

"I know the animals are going to be killed but that is a shame. I would kill Parliament if he was an animal. I think you can't close the zoo and kill the animals."—Jacqueline MacKay.

● Teacher Linda Keith spells out her pupils' message to the council.

of a meeting held on 17th February 1977. Again, all of this was played out in the local press.

By August 1977 the decision was taken to close the Zoo at the end of the month, 11 years after it opened.

In November 1977 a Society meeting recorded the disposal of animals as noted below:

Ravensden Zoological Company Ltd	agouti, wildcat, civet, guanaco, kinkajou, macaque, seal, puma, alligator, boa constrictor, pelican, cassowary
Aberdeen District	birds
Cleethorpes Zoo	dingo (2) lion (3) wolf (3)
Chester Zoo	agouti (1) dingo (2) chimpanzee (2)
Not Known	bear

In these final dispatches the Society acknowledged the commitment and dedication shown by the staff and it was agreed to pay them a small bonus. In the same spirit it was agreed to waive any rent and rates owed by the Leslies for the house since April.

Bruno the bear leaving the Zoo when it closed in 1977

I hope I have shown that the demise of the Zoo was not a straightforward and inevitable conclusion, but the cumulative effect of a series of decisions and circumstances which had a profound effect. The decision to locate at Hazlehead, the change in office bearers at Aberdeen City Council, the amount of Zoo management time trying to procure additional land and the shortage of funds all conspired to bring about the demise of the Zoo. As I reflect on these issues I wonder if perhaps the Society was not ambitious enough. It would certainly have benefited from a high-profile sponsor. Who knows what might have been?

As a result of the above the Society went into administration in August 1977 and the Zoo, which had been the source of enjoyment and education, ceased to exist.

How do you Measure Success?

In these days of spin, alternative facts and fake news it is easy to be cynical when someone says how successful they are. I do not claim that Aberdeen Zoo was the best, biggest or most successful Zoo, but I would like to highlight some of the things it did well, which may influence your judgement.

If you consider the numbers game, the Zoo had 10,000 visitors in its first weekend. Indeed, the Zoo had to be closed to visitors because the paths and buildings were filled to capacity. Trying to lift a choc ice without apologising to the person next to you was impossible! During the first few weeks, from the 16th July until 29th August 1966, there were 72,000 visitors.

The quarter millionth visitor, a girl from Edinburgh, entered the Zoo in November 1967 and was given a set of 16 volumes of 'The Encyclopaedia of Animals' to mark the occasion.

Given the population of Aberdeen, the numbers visiting the Zoo are quite impressive.

The Society wished to keep interested members of the public informed, and to achieve this they had both Senior and Junior Zoo Clubs. These were set up even before the Zoo was opened. In the late 60s and early 70s the Senior Zoo Club had 200 members and the Junior Zoo Club had in excess of 350 members. These were active and engaged members, as can be seen by the 200 children who attended a talk by Captain Newton on his time as a game warden in Uganda. This was not a one-off spike in attendance, as it was noted at the AGM in 1965 that the average attendance at the monthly meetings was 250. What organisation today would not be jealous of managing to attract so many youngsters?

To illustrate this key priority of the Zoo, my father was invited to a conference on 'Education in Zoos', held in Amsterdam. Aberdeen Zoo had been recognised as one of the best 28 zoos in Europe for its educational programme. This was despite

Join the Junior Zoo Club . . .

THE next meeting of the Junior Zoo Club is on Tuesday, January 5, at 7 p.m., in the Girl Guide HQ, 11 Albyn Place, Aberdeen. Meet Ringo, the honey badger.

There is also the second round of the Inter-school Zoo Quiz. Entry is free to members — you can join the club at all meetings.

Now about a future event— dance to the "Misfits" at the Badger's Ball on January 9, at Kirk House, Belmont Street, from 8-11.30 p.m. Tickets (4/-) from Publicity Office, Union Street, or at Zoo Club meeting.

Kids start 'zoo week'

More than 60 children took part in a nature hunt at Nigg Bay—to start the Aberdeen and North-east Zoological Society's "Zoo Week."

The children were divided into six teams and had to find as many forms of life as possible in the rocks and rock pools. The winning group collected 20 different species.

having been open for only three years.

On opening the Zoo, Peter Scott commented that the Zoo was the most interesting in the world due in part to its ethos and commitment to education.

In May 1968 the local press questioned whether we were 'Too Modest About our Zoo', and chastised the Zoo for not applying for membership of the Federation of Zoological Gardens of Great Britain and Ireland. My father, in response, cited the shortage of additional land for isolation units or an animal hospital. These were mandatory requirements for membership. My father stated that there was not much point in lodging an application and paying the expenses for a visitation from the assessors, only to fail as the Zoo could not satisfy what was a basic requirement for membership. This recurrent theme of land availability had dogged the Zoo since the very beginning, and influenced so many things from the possible procurement of an elephant to the ultimate demise of the Zoo.

Despite this lack of land, the Management of Aberdeen Zoo did wish to join the Federation; in fact, it was recognised that this was critical. There were numerous communications between the Federation and the Zoo. Indeed, Geoffrey Schomberg, the secretary of the Federation, visited Aberdeen in 1969 to inspect the Zoo. He was made aware of the situation with regard to the shortage of hospital and isolation units which were as a result of the physical limitations of the site.

The Zoo also played its part in international conservation efforts. An example was recorded in a letter from the National Swedish Environment Protection Board. In this 'warmest thanks' were conveyed to the Zoo for its part in transferring Scottish peregrine falcons to Sweden to augment their population.

If visitor numbers are not a measure of success, how about breeding successes? Animals will not breed if they do not have the right conditions.

The Zoo was recognised as a leader in breeding grey seals in captivity. The grey seal colony, acknowledged as the best kept in Britain, produced a grey seal pup, born on Christmas Day 1972. Aberdeen was only the second zoo in Britain, after London, and the sixth in the world to achieve this. This success was recorded in two scientific papers 'Observations on the Grey Seal at Aberdeen Zoo' (Halichoerus grypus) and 'Breeding of Grey Seals at Aberdeen Zoo', written by my father. Both were published in the International Zoo Yearbook Volumes 11 and 14, 1971 and 1974 respectively.

The Zoo also had success in breeding Scottish wildcats (Felis silvestris grampia), which was recorded in my father's paper in the International Zoo Yearbook Volume 12 in 1972.

Malayan fruit bats (Cynopterus brachyotis) also bred in the Zoo and again featured in a paper in the International Zoo Yearbook Volume 11 in 1971.

A note on the honey buzzard (Pernis apivorus) also received recognition and inclusion in the International Zoo Yearbook Volume 10 in 1970.

Perhaps the greatest achievement was the first recorded breeding of Oriental short-clawed otters in captivity for which my father received the Gavin Maxwell Award on the 15th June 1972. The species was also the subject of two papers: one titled 'Observations on the Oriental short-clawed otter (Aonyx cinerea) published in the International Zoo Yearbook Volume 10 in 1970 and the other 'Further Observations on the Oriental short-clawed otter (Aonyx cinerea) published in the International Zoo Yearbook Volume 11 in 1971.

In addition to the successes outlined above, the breeding of pig-tailed macaques was an acknowledged achievement in a letter from the Society to Aberdeen City Council, written in January 1973. It was also noted that the Zoo was only one of three British zoos which had managed to breed wolves. The letter went on to note that badgers, ravens, barn owls and myna birds, which were termed as 'difficult to breed species', had been bred in the Zoo. Some of the 'easier' species such as dingoes, wallabies and red deer had all successfully bred.

The letter also highlighted the success of the grey seal colony with regard to the orphaned and injured seal pups which had been brought to the Zoo. Twenty-four of the 29 pups brought to the Zoo survived.

Some measure success by how they are judged by their peers. I have already quoted Peter Scott, but I will add the testament of J.L. Thorp, Director of Honolulu Zoo, who visited 18 zoos and animal parks in Great Britain and Ireland in 1973.

'If I could make a composite zoo of the best features of the 18 zoos and animal parks I visited in the British Isles and Ireland this summer and have it located in a community of my choice, this is what I would have......

From Aberdeen - to begin with, I would just take the whole of Hazlehead Park, George Leslie's red hair and accent. Probably the single most interesting exhibit was the Scottish wildcat display.

In conclusion, I regret that there are many zoos and animal parks that I missed during this long, but too short a stay in the British Isles and Ireland. The 'Composite Zoo' must necessarily do without the treasures from these gardens until my next visit.

And one final thought. I would hope that I could retain your professional friendship even though I covet your grandest accomplishments in our field'.

It is difficult after all these years to measure the level of success for a fledging zoo with limited funds and a constant battle with its landlords over expansion. However, all I can remember is the caring nature of all who worked at the Zoo. The welfare of the animals came first, and everyone did their utmost to give the animals in their care as comfortable an environment as possible.

All in all, an impressive record for such a young zoo.

Aberdeen Zoo in winter

Children's Corner

Part Two - Introducing the Animals

The definition of a zoo, according to Wikipedia, is a facility in which all animals are housed within enclosures displayed to the public, and in which they may also breed.

The animals are therefore of primary importance; without them you have no zoo.

Despite its small size, approximately two acres, the Zoo packed in a lot of animals. According to the entry in the International Zoo Year Book Volume 12, published in 1972, the Zoo contained 73 species of mammal with 194 specimens, 120 species of bird with 420 specimens, 9 species of reptile with 38 specimens; a total of 257 species and 873 specimens including fish and invertebrates.

It is not possible, or perhaps not very interesting for the reader, to describe all these species. I have therefore included anecdotes on some of my personal favourites and also some which were newsworthy for various reasons. As I mentioned in the introduction, my father had started to write a book about the Zoo. Initially I had intended transcribing these chapters into my own words, but I felt it would be more fitting to include his own words as a legacy and to mark his commitment to the establishment and the running of Aberdeen Zoo (Part Three).

An intriguing and valid question would be how do you stock a zoo once you have decided to build one? You can't very well stroll down to your local Tesco or B&Q with a list – I'll have a pair of those donkeys and while you are at it do you have any dingoes on offer, three for the price of two or buy one get one free?

As I have suggested previously, we were living in different times back in the early 60s. People were returning to Britain from overseas postings around the world bringing back all sorts of animals. These ranged from snakes to monkeys, chimpanzees to bears and everything else in between. This was quite acceptable back then, as there was little by way of regulation, certainly no CITES (Convention on International Trade in Endangered Species). The Zoo was thus offered all manner of species from leopards from India, red river hogs from Nigeria, parrots and ornamental pheasants, monkeys, a chimpanzee and even a Pyrenean mountain dog! This dog hadn't been brought back from abroad, but had simply become too big for its owner. Before the Zoo was a physical reality these animals posed the tricky problem of finding temporary accommodation which I have covered elsewhere.

In addition to these animal donations, some bequests were made to buy a specific animal and between the two sources the Zoo was stocked.

Once the Zoo was a going concern, the Society constantly assessed the animals to see if they were suitable for the Zoo. If it was thought that any animal would be better in another establishment, perhaps for breeding purposes, then this was done. As an example, a palm civet was sent to London Zoo to add to its breeding programme. In some cases, the Zoo had been successful in breeding some of its animals leading to a surplus. These could then be sold or swapped with other zoos. I remember going down to Flamingo Land and Twycross Zoo with my father to deliver grey seals.

In 1971 my father embarked on a 'Zoo Tour', as it was referred to in the minutes of a Society meeting. On this Tour my father took red deer to Peterborough, a wildcat to Weyhill, four-horned sheep to Bristol, and ravens to St Albans. He did not return empty handed as he picked up a long-haired Malayan sun bear in Portland, a monkey and a cassowary from Edinburgh and a kinkajou from Dundee. During this 'mammoth' trip, he visited establishments at Riber Castle, Longleat, Rode Bird Gardens, Bristol Zoo, Paignton Zoo, Bourton-on-the-Water and Twycross Zoo. It was a fairly major expedition undertaken to glean information on animal husbandry, find out about opportunities to barter or sell animals and to generally increase the Zoo's network of contacts.

It was not just British zoos that Aberdeen Zoo had dealings with. When it became clear that the Zoo was not going to receive Gavin Maxwell's otters, the Zoo investigated the possibility of obtaining penguins to fill the area which had been prepared for the otters. Bob Laing, one of the members of the Society, was tasked with making contact with San Diego and Los Angeles Zoos to ascertain whether any penguins were available. Unfortunately, there is no record of the outcome.

It was also quite understandable that after Dr Lil de Kock moved to Germany, contacts would be forthcoming with German zoos. This saw the exchange of grey seals from Aberdeen in return for pelicans from Nuremburg Zoo, which also offered a pair of snowy owls.

One of the Zoo's stated objectives was to exhibit indigenous animals that could still be found in the British Isles, or which had previously been resident in the country, for example bears and wolves.

Enclosures were built to house animals such as Scottish wildcats and wolves. However, some of these animals proved problematic. It must have seemed a good idea to have badgers at the Zoo; they were, after all, the animal featured in the logo of the Zoo. Undoubtedly, the powers that be knew that badgers were predominantly nocturnal. A fairly large enclosure was constructed to house these animals. Unfortunately, the badgers hadn't got the memo about changing their habits to show a waiting public their humbug-striped faces. Many an hour was spent by the public looking forlornly into the enclosure, but to no avail. In fact, the only time they were seen was by the various keepers who were working late into the evening. The badgers had to go!

I remember spending my school holidays working alongside some off-duty firemen to convert the badger enclosure into an area more suitable for pumas. This involved creating a collar to go round the large tree, which was the centre piece of the enclosure in order to allow a roof of chain link to be constructed. Your average puma is a bit more adept at climbing than your sleepy badger. The conversion was eventually

finished and the pumas were acquired and moved in. The puma enclosure was the site of what could have been the Zoo's most horrific and fatal accident. As well as the full-time keepers the Zoo was staffed by many volunteers, young boys and girls who worked under the supervision of the keepers. One day a young boy took it upon himself to go in to the puma enclosure, either with food or to do some cleaning. The alarm was raised and my father and the keepers ran to the enclosure to find the young boy trying to climb the tree with the aid of his shoulder blades, while a fierce puma took a swipe and removed the glasses from his face. Thankfully, the boy did not turn his back on the puma otherwise the outcome could have been so different. The keepers came in through the two security gates and managed to extricate the boy from the enclosure without either people or animals being harmed. I cannot remember the boy's name but I am sure he can remember the day he stood nose to nose with a puma and lived to tell the tale.

One of the indigenous species the Zoo wished to exhibit was wild boar. Mr Ferguson, a pig breeder from the New Pitsligo area, was generous in subsidising the purchase of wild boar piglets. The piglets duly arrived, and I can attest to the difficulty in catching the little blighters. We thought we only had to open the trailer and gently guide them into the prepared enclosure. The piglets had other ideas and shot out of the travelling cage at about 40 miles per hour. Have you ever tried to catch a sleek little rocket which is down at knee height, at a speed which would give Usain Bolt a problem?

John Buchan with wild boars, Percy and Pauline

Thankfully, the operation was carried out after hours, when the public were not there to witness our comedic efforts as the two piglets ran amok. I remember Harvey Smith, one of the keepers, diving out of the way as one of the piglets hurtled towards me. Eventually the two runaways were coerced into their awaiting enclosure. Percy and Pauline, as they were named, made their home for many years in the enclosure. This it must be said looked a bit scruffy, as it contained a mud bath to help keep their skin and feet in good condition.

As has been emphasised, one of the aims of the Zoo was to educate, and to this end there were notice boards informing the public about the animal in the exhibit. However, you cannot guarantee anyone will read them! One day my father came back to the house apoplectic about a man he had overheard at the wild boar enclosure saying to his children that it was a pity that the polar bears were so dirty. So much for the signage!

Wolves were to be found in the British Isles until people managed to eradicate them. The last is said to have been shot in Badenoch in 1743.

The Zoo had a pack of wolves in one enclosure and it was easy to forget they were wild animals as they loped round. They appeared afraid of humans and would not come too close to anyone mucking out their quarters. Like many animals which are kept in captivity they became almost domesticated. However, that did not stop them trying to get out. I remember coming home to be told that one of the wolves, which had been in a quarantine cage, had chewed its way out and was somewhere in the Zoo. I entered the Zoo with a bit of trepidation, as I was not sure if I was going to

Dad with one of the wolves

be confronted with a scared animal which was about the size of an Alsatian dog on steroids. Thankfully, it turned out to be at the west end of the Zoo where a posse of keepers, along with my father, was trying to encourage the wayward animal back into its enclosure. We found out that night that wolves do not like black polythene sheeting. One of the keepers sat on top of the back gate, trying not to do himself an

injury on the barbed wire, whilst rustling a large roll of polythene to dissuade the beast from making a leap for freedom over the gate. This was a fair jump for a wolf, but we did not want to find out if it was possible. Eventually, the wolf was safely back in the enclosure with its kin and no worse for its adventure, unlike the staff who were all panting after their exertions.

As I said before, it was sometimes easy to forget that these were wild animals. One day a keeper steadied herself as she went between the enclosures by putting her rubber-gloved hand against the chain link fence. The wolves either thought someone was being playful, or had put some food through the wire, and grabbed at the fingers, removing part of the glove along with the tip of the finger. This was upsetting enough, but it was compounded by the fact that the keeper, Mrs Wainwright, was an accomplished pianist and this incident had a debilitating effect on her ability to play.

African Grey Parrot

There were a few African grey parrots which had been donated to the Zoo; most ended up in the free flight aviary. However, now and again a bird arrived which had been so fixated by human company that it was obvious that it would not do well in the aviary. Birds from the parrot family would pluck out their feathers through either stress or boredom. Solomon Roger was donated to the Zoo and it was obvious from his repertoire that he had been in human company too long. It was decided therefore that he would come and stay in our house at the Zoo. He was a real character who could announce his name in imperious style. When he heard the noise of cooking, and us sitting down to eat, you would hear 'Chips Solomon' coming from the living room. He would then make a noise like someone scraping a plate. But perhaps his funniest trick was summoning Moira, my father's sheepdog. Moira had been given to my father at the Mart by a shepherd who could no longer house her. Moira's spartan working existence suddenly took a step towards the finer things in life. My father had a unique whistle to summon Moira which Solomon soon mastered. It was comical, when my father was out, to hear Solomon whistle to Moira who dutifully came running through to the living room. When my father was nowhere to be seen, Moira would return to her bed. He had also mastered the art of comic timing and just as Moira settled down, he would whistle again, causing Moira to immediately come back to the living room. Solomon could keep this up for some considerable time, which was good as it helped reduce Moira's rather rotund figure. After the Zoo closed, I am pleased to say that mum and dad were allowed to keep Solomon and he was a cherished family pet until he finally passed away.

Free flight aviary

Agoutis

Agoutis are rodents native to South America and are known to be very timid creatures that can become extremely distressed when confronted by humans. Agoutis are mainly nocturnal, but it was reported in the press that the ones inhabiting the free flight aviary had been reared in Bavaria by Konrad Lorenz and had been conditioned to give up the night life. I recall the agoutis running about the aviary during the day much to the delight of the public.

Arctic Foxes

Arctic foxes are one of those animals which have a lovely thick silver-blue coat in winter; the reason that many were kept in captivity for the fur trade. In summer however they cast their lovely coat and were what could only be described as scruffy. I wondered if this was one of the species which David Welch, Director of Links and Parks, referred to when he said that *'some animals were not particularly attractive at all times of the year especially when shedding their coats'*. However, that is nature and I am sure there are times when we humans don't look our best.

Bears

To illustrate how circumstances have changed, there is no better story than how Dainty, the Malayan sun bear, ended up in a zoo in Aberdeen.

Dainty was born in the mountainous regions of Vietnam and at the age of approximately three weeks old was found abandoned by two American Servicemen. She was given to 10-year old Annabel Helmore, daughter of the British Air Attaché in Saigon, Group Captain Peter Helmore.

Dainty was brought up by the Helmores as a family pet, but she eventually had to be excluded from the house as she just caused chaos. She was kept in a large dog kennel which she managed to chew her way out of. In the middle of the night she would climb up the outside of the house and ask to be let in through the bedroom window.

When Dainty was two years old the Helmores moved from Vietnam and returned to the South of England. Dainty was such a close family pet that she could not be left behind as Vietnam was in the throes of war, so she was flown to Singapore and then put on a cargo boat bound for England. During the long voyage she was exercised by the crew who took her round the boat on a lead.

Once in England she was so dependent on humans she had to be housed in an enclosure in the Helmore's garden. Various attempts were made to introduce other bears for company, but to no avail. Mrs Helmore and her daughter ended up moving to Ballater and thought it would be best if they lent Dainty to Aberdeen Zoo. She soon settled in, and the Helmores could continue to visit. Not exactly a Paddington-type story, but representative of a time when the movement of animals was far less restricted. We now realise that without these restrictions man would seek to exploit the animal kingdom to such an extent that many more species would be extinct.

Dainty and Bruno

It was considered important to find a mate for Dainty as she was six years old. After a bit of a search a potential mate was found in Portland, Dorset. Bruno was a family pet who at the age of two and half had outgrown his family surroundings and was available. My father and John Buchan drove to Portland and, after a bit of fun and games trying to get the bear into a suitable travel cage, they succeeded and brought Bruno back to Aberdeen and Dainty. Thankfully, the two hit it off and settled down to life in Aberdeen.

Dainty and Bruno were popular with the public. It may have been something to do with the fact that they were associated with a well-known breakfast cereal advertisement campaign. At that time 'Jeremy the Sugar Puff bear' was all over the media and it was reported Bruno was the original 'Jeremy', although I cannot verify this fact. Many of the children thought that these bears were cuddly and insisted on reaching over the barrier fence to try and get close. The local newspapers carried an article warning children that the bears they saw in the adverts were young cubs and the adult bears were capable of tearing their arms from their sockets. A bit extreme if you like, but anything short of this would have been ignored.

As a postscript to the story, the newspapers told of the darker side of using 'wild animals' in advertisement campaigns as they were disposed of when they became too big or unruly to be used safely. I remember being told that chimpanzees could only be used in circuses and travelling menageries up to the age of seven years after which they would be too strong to be controlled.

Birds - Exotic

The free flight aviary was loosely styled on other zoo buildings throughout the world, and in particular Frankfurt Zoo. It was cutting edge in its time. The aviary was home to many species of birds from mynas to manakins and turacos to toucans, and was very popular as a place to just sit and reflect as exotic birds flew over your head. Many of these birds were donated by Alf Robertson from Dundee.

As the Zoo plans were being formulated, he offered to donate his collection of birds to the Zoo. I remember going down to Dundee, armed with varying sizes of catching nets and crates of all shapes

Blue and Yellow Macaw and sizes, to catch and transport the birds back to

Greater Necklaced Laughingthrush

Aberdeen. From what I recall we entered the aviaries and caught the birds as they flew at a great rate of knots up and down the aviary. Having learnt how to catch various animals I had become quite adept at catching the birds in what were oversized butterfly nets. The trick was to let the birds fly into the net and, with a quick flick of the wrist, turn the frame of the net round to trap the bird in the bottom of the net. It depended on the type of bird, but most were fairly easy to handle. Parakeets and parrots posed more of a challenge. If you have ever had to catch a budgerigar you will know that they can inflict an amazingly sore nip. I remember when I worked at Scorgie's Pet Store in Rose Street the look of puzzlement on the client's face as I had my hand with a budgie in the small carrying box and I didn't seem to be doing anything.

What they did not realise was the little blighter had hold of the soft flap of skin between my thumb and palm. It was up to the bird when you could extract your hand. Parakeets and parrots take the risk factor to a different level, inflicting serious bites including the removal of substantial chunks of your digits. Remember, some of the parrot species can crack the shells of formidable nuts and woe betide if it was a macaw you were dealing with as all your fingers were in danger. The birds were safely transported to Aberdeen and formed the nucleus of the collection of birds to be found around the Zoo. Alf Robertson and his wife became regular callers to the Zoo to catch up with my parents and to see how their birds were faring.

African Crowned Crane

Black Swans

The arrival of two black swans highlights the inter-zoo trade. One grey seal was swapped for two black swans. The article in the local press carried the headline 'a Worthwhile Equation'. I remember heading south with my father in the Ford Thames van filled with animals which we were taking to several English zoos. The black swans were from Flamingo Land. I remember getting to stroke Cuddles, the killer whale. I was also offered a job, as my upbringing had revolved so much around animals. I had accumulated a decent amount of knowledge regarding animal husbandry. However, I declined. I was not sure I wanted a career with animals.

Capercaillie

In an early meeting of the Society in October 1962, it was noted that two female capercaillie had been donated by a gamekeeper and these two birds were at Foresterhill.

I remember going up on to the roof at the Medical School at Foresterhill Hospital. I was carrying larch and heather shoots which my father had collected from the outskirts of Aberdeen to feed the two birds which were kept in a large cage. When a male was brought in after it had been found in Kirkhill Forest, there was hope that it would mate with the females. Unfortunately, he had been attacked by a fox or a dog, was badly injured and never recovered.

Cassowary

Keeper Ray Slaven and Cassowary

The cassowary was labelled a 'killer bird' to try and deter egg collectors. The crowned cranes shared an enclosure with the cassowary. When the cranes had laid their eggs, thieves climbed the fence and stole them. A newspaper article highlighted the reputation that cassowaries have for using their rather large feet to kick anyone who was threatening them, sometimes with fatal consequences.

Chimpanzees

Undoubtedly the most charismatic of all the animals I remember at the Zoo was Humphrey, the chimpanzee. I have left my father to tell Humphrey's story, but I feel that I should add a couple of comments. He was a cheeky chap and incredibly strong for such a small creature. As he grew and I carried him about the Zoo, I used to effectively bear-hug him, wrapping my arms around his body and locking my hands behind him. I had inherited some of my father's strength and this, together with undertaking manual work at the Zoo, meant I was relatively strong. However, chimps have the advantage of not only a pair of hands, but a pair of very dexterous feet which Humphrey used to great effect. He would pummel your stomach or sometimes the area that boxers would refer to as 'below the belt'. Carrying Humphrey around could be a painful experience.

When Humphrey was misbehaving in the house my father would physically restrain him, Humphrey remembered this and respected the fact that my father could restrain him, even though he surpassed the strength of us mere humans. How strong was Humphrey? Well when he and his mate Heather were in their purpose-built enclosure, I remember seeing Humphrey dangling from the roof structure by one finger. He then lifted John Buchan, the Head Keeper, off the ground using his feet. The total weight was probably between 15 and 20 stone supported by one finger - impressive! You daren't give either chimp a pan with a handle on it as they would just twist off the handle no matter how strong the fixings.

Humphrey was perhaps the most photogenic of all the animals at the Zoo. I remember him in the house, and I defy anyone to look into a chimp's eyes and not see an intelligence there.

Newspaper articles featured Humphrey inspecting his new enclosure with Heather - Humphrey the pickpocket who managed to lift the keys from the keeper's pocket and hide them; Humphrey the photographer trying to use an old camera before getting fed up and breaking it. He was always up for a party and was pictured celebrating various birthdays. Indeed, it seems he also gate-crashed a party being held by the Odeon Cinema Children's Club. He also thanked the public who donated bananas when they were in short supply following a dock strike in 1972.

Humphrey also featured extensively in the April Fools' Day phone calls where many were

John Buchan and Humphrey

directed to Mr Humphrey. In the pre-Amazon era books, rug making samples and football pools were all ordered on behalf of Mr Humphrey. It was not unusual for the Zoo to receive 250 calls on 1st April.

During a hunt for a mate the black market in chimps was highlighted, and it is sad to say that we still hear reports in the media of animals being inhumanely trafficked by greedy people.

One advantage I had in living at the Zoo was that I had a ready supply of exhibits for any talks I had to give as part of my English classes at Summerhill School. Humphrey was one of my 'props' and the fact that I passed the Spoken English exam was more to do with everyone paying more attention to Humphrey than to my talk.

Dad and Heather

Dad, Mum and Humphrey at home

Chipmunks

In the section written by my father on escaped animals, he didn't mention the two chipmunks which escaped from the GPO office at Joint Station. Unfortunately, George Taylor, the Head Clerk, managed to get himself bitten and had to get an anti-tetanus injection, which probably was as painful as the bite. My father was also bitten, but shrugged it off saying he was immune to that sort of thing. He always claimed he was never bitten; all I can say it was a good thing his name was not Pinocchio!

Donkeys

Donkeys, Ferrie and Etna

The animals at the Zoo were used in all kinds of publicity shoots. A donkey was used as a prop when Pierre de Kock, representing the World Wildlife Fund, met representatives from VG Stores. They had promised to donate £100,000 per year, over the next few years, towards saving the wildlife of Britain, which aligned with the Zoo's original ethos to show indigenous animals.

The donkeys also featured in an article in August 1970 which stated that '*the Zoo at Hazlehead is undoubtedly one of the holiday attractions without which Aberdeen would be the poorer*'.

Dingoes

Dingoes were a popular exhibit at the Zoo; they could be seen from both outside and also from the corridor in the Tropical House. One of the original dingoes, Taffy, was purchased from the Welsh Mountain Zoo. The dingoes generally settled in well and proved quite easy to breed.

Dingo Postcard

In fact, one of the articles in the press showed Valerie Turner, one of the keepers, holding some dingo pups and asking if anyone wanted to buy six of them.

I am not a particularly squeamish person, but my loathing of maggots goes back to

Keeper Valerie Turner and Dingoes

110

the time when I was clearing out the dingo enclosure. I have mentioned elsewhere that when sheep were injured in transit to the Mart they were put down and used by the Zoo as food for the various carnivores. After the dingoes had had their fill, the carcass had to be removed. Often as it was disturbed, it was found to be writhing with maggots. It was not a pleasant experience and one which put you off your curry with rice.

Although the dingoes generally got along, I remember when one new male was introduced to the pack. The dominant male was not happy, but did not attack the newcomer straight away. The attack came later, and the new male had to be put down as the dominant male had effectively castrated the poor beast.

I cannot be sure, but one of the males from the litters did not fancy having the same fate and it escaped. It was seen in the countryside around Monymusk and Tilliefourie. The poor beast was eventually tracked down at Rhynie, but was in such poor condition it had to be put down.

Ferret

Ferrets are not particularly exciting beasts, but an article from 1976 caught my eye. 'Justice' was administered in a more direct way during the 1960s and 70s; something we would not condone or accept today. Imagine when two young lads stole a ferret, and were sent back to the Zoo by their parents. To make amends the two lads were given the rather smelly task of cleaning out the manure cart. I bet they never stole another ferret or probably anything else in their life. Maybe this direct approach where parents take responsibility and children are taught true values has something to commend it.

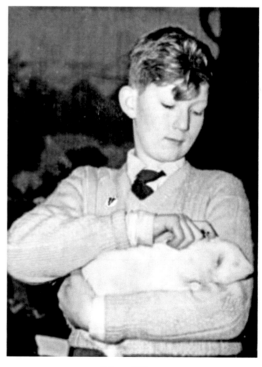

Me and Ferret
(note the Junior Zoo Club badge)

Flamingo

The arrival of one of these birds in 1976 was unusual. A flamingo was found caught up on the nets which covered the helicopter deck of a North Sea oil rig. The bird was put in a box and transported to the Zoo.

Unfortunately, the local yobs targeted this bird and threw either a stick or stone which broke its leg. Efforts were made to support the flamingo by using a part of a golf club shaft to support the leg while it healed. Unfortunately, this did not work, and the bird died. This story was used to highlight the rising amount of vandalism encountered in 1975/76. There was even an incident where a young boy was caught with a pheasant up his jumper which he was going to pass to his father who was waiting around the corner to wring its neck, as it was destined to be their Sunday lunch!

Goats

I have tried to give you a flavour of the Zoo and, talking of flavours, one of the reasons I don't particularly like goat's cheese is as a result of Little Billy. He was an African tree-climbing goat. He was one of the first animals donated to the Zoo and was kept by Mr Coopey. If memory serves me right, he was a camera man with BBC TV, and lived on Garthdee Road. When we took the animals to the various highland games and shows with the aim of raising funds, Little Billy was one of the exhibits. He was transported in the back of my father's van. He was not house trained and definitely not van trained. After you have spent an hour or so in the closed environment of the van with his strong-smelling urine and 'poo', you wouldn't like goat's cheese either!

Fox

The lower part of the Zoo, next to the entrance to our house, contained many of the animals which were child friendly. Here you would find lambs and donkeys, but by far the most charismatic character was Foxie, the red fox. He had been donated to the Zoo after being hand reared. He had a collar which was attached to a running lead. This meant he had quite a lot of free movement. As soon as he recognised myself or any of the other keepers he would come straight over to the low fence and prostrate himself. He was just as friendly as any domesticated dog, and as well as tickling him I would not hesitate to grab his muzzle and let him put his teeth around my hands and fingers. He was taken for walks round Hazlehead Park by the keepers.

I did get bitten by one fox. One day a gentleman brought a fox to the Zoo in a wicker basket with the intention of donating it. A dog's lead protruded from the basket which he grabbed as he opened the basket. He had not realised it had done a Harry Houdini on him. A bemused gentleman was left holding a lead as this little red rocket took off out of the Zoo towards the potting sheds. The frightened beast was cornered by myself and another couple of keepers. I grabbed it by the scruff of the neck. I did not hold it tightly enough as the fox squirmed round and tried to fillet my finger. Thankfully we managed to restrain the poor beast and get it securely housed.

Grey Squirrels

Jack

I have a confession to make on behalf of the Zoo. It appears that the Zoo was responsible for all the grey squirrels which can be found in and around the North East of Scotland. How do I come to this conclusion?

Back in March 1971 the Zoo was offered between 12 and 20 grey squirrels from Weyhill in England. The grey squirrels arrived in June 1971. Grey squirrels are undoubtedly cute, but they have a devastating effect on the indigenous red squirrel population. As an exhibit they were fairly active and the young children loved their antics, but they could hardly be called exotic.

When the Zoo was being wound up in 1977 there is a record of only one grey squirrel remaining. So what happened to the rest? They either all died bar one or they escaped.

I attended a talk in 2016 by Steven Willis from the Saving Scotland's Red Squirrel campaign. He noted that the grey squirrels found in the North East of Scotland were an 'island' population extending north from the city to about Peterhead, but going no further south than the Mearns area. The DNA samples taken from the North East population of grey squirrels are distinct from those found in the squirrels in the Dundee and Fife areas. They are more akin to those found in the grey squirrels of the New Forest area in England. Guess where Weyhill is?

I doubt if you will need a second guess.

Gyrfalcon

As a bird watcher I would love to see a gyrfalcon in the wild. A trip to Iceland saw me dip out on this species. It would seem that these birds do come close to our

Dad, John Buchan and Gyrfalcon

114

shores as the Zoo ended up with two gyrfalcons which were handed in over the years. One was found exhausted and contaminated with oil on the Ocean Rover in the Forties Field, located about 130 miles north east of Aberdeen.

My father identified the bird as a white-phase gyrfalcon which could have attracted a price of £1,000 as they are much prized by falconers. The bird had to be decontaminated and this required an almost 24 hour a day ritual of cleansing to rid the feathers of the oils. Unfortunately, I can find no record of the fate of the bird, but I assume that every effort was made to return it to the wild. However, if the bird was in such a condition that it would not survive, then it would have been well looked after at the Zoo.

Incredibly another gyrfalcon ended up at the Zoo. The exhausted bird landed on the Aberdeen-based Grampian Monarch fishing boat and was brought back to Aberdeen. The bird was nursed back to health. During that period it was reported that Roy Dennis, who was then part of the RSPB's Operation Osprey at Loch Garten, came over to Aberdeen to see the bird as he had never seen one before. Once the bird was back to health it was flown by BEA to Shetland where another 'well-kent' face in birding circles, Bobby Tulloch, took possession of the bird and released it back into the wild.

Gibbons

Monk, the gibbon, taking a rest

The tragic story of the two grey gibbons was featured in the press. Monk, the male gibbon, died when he ingested a plastic bag. Fifty-odd years later we are just realising the legacy that plastic has left us with. It was reported under the headline 'The Faithfulness of the Gibbon' that his mate Mimi died of a broken heart.

Undoubtedly, this cannot really be proved but a post-mortem on Mimi uncovered no apparent cause of death.

To replace Monk, the Zoo acquired Sparky who was a bit of a character.

Apes and primates are funny creatures, as they will allow you to play with them, but they soon let you know when you have outstayed your welcome. I remember Sparky used to really like having his back scratched. When he saw me coming up the path, he would immediately come to the edge of his enclosure and spin round on his long arms until his back was pressed up against the wire. I would scratch away and he would enjoy the attention, and then he would suddenly spin round and snap at my fingers.

If I still wanted to be able to count to 10, I had to remember that most things bite and had to remain vigilant.

In another demonstration of his changing temperament, I saw Sparky reach out and grab a pheasant chick. The pheasant eggs had been incubated by a hen, and the hen and its adopted

Sparky

brood had managed to get in behind the outer safety fence and the gibbons' enclosure. Sparky gently stroked the chick and looked with a loving expression at the ball of feathers in his hand. Sparky then decided that the chick did not hold any more attraction for him and at this point he flicked his thumb and broke the poor chick's neck.

Kinkajous

Despite the fact that kinkajous look cuddly, like little teddy bears, they can be wicked little blighters. They were one of the few animals in the Zoo that managed to catch me out and inflict some bites.

When I was putting food into their enclosure one of the cuddly little things dropped down from the roof on its prehensile tail whilst, in a coordinated pincer attack, one started climbing up my legs, biting through my trousers. A quick flick of my hand and a swift kick managed to dislodge both of the beasts. They were none the worse from the skirmish, but I had to go and wash my wounds in a Dettol bath.

They were another breeding success for the Zoo.

Lions

The decision to obtain three lion cubs in place of the much hoped-for elephant was not universally welcomed. However, the three cubs were generally well received and featured heavily in the press. The lions were named MacNicol, Leila and Victoria.

MacNicol when she arrived at the zoo as a cub

The third of the cubs, Victoria, was three months old when she arrived at the Zoo. She had been hand-reared at Longleat by Mary Chipperfield. Jimmy Chipperfield then flew the cub to Glasgow in his private plane. My father drove to Glasgow to pick up the cub. Like so many of the young animals which arrived at the Zoo they were to be found living in our house, which led to many an interesting encounter.

MacNicol (named after keeper John Buchan whose middle name was MacNicol) was born in Glasgow Zoo and collected by my father in 1974. It was reported that MacNicol was poorly and cold on the way back from Glasgow despite being tucked into my father's shirt - a detour to a hotel in Perth was called for. Now it is not clear whether my father needed a nip of whisky, but he did give the cold cub a drink of whisky from his fingers. The barmaid is reputed to have queried whether she was being set up by Candid Camera when MacNicol was produced. The cub made it back to Aberdeen where it was given five feeds of Jersey cow milk, one every four hours to replace its mother's milk.

Sometime later local journalist, Ruth Morrison, paid a visit to the Zoo and was pictured in the enclosure with MacNicol, who was a fairly big cat by this time. Ruth admitted to being nervous and it was at this point my father claimed that there was no such thing as a wild animal and in all his years in dealing with them he had never been bitten. What a fibber!

Scottish personalities visited the Zoo and actress Molly Weir featured an article about meeting MacNicol in one of her columns.

MacNicol at nine months old weighing in at nearly ten stone

Children helping to raise money with Leila

You can only imagine the embarrassment of the staff, especially my father, when it eventually transpired that MacNicol was not King of the Jungle but Queen. Although the Zoo were sold the tiny MacNicol as a male, the lack of mane some years later called for some closer investigation. So much for the breeding prospects when it turned out that the Zoo had three female lions. The cubs were also used to help publicise local events. Leila helped with the World Wildlife Fund collecting effort and the opening of the PDSA Shop in George Street, Aberdeen.

Llamas and Guanacos

Guanaco Panji with Jiji who was bred at the Zoo

The Zoo had exhibits of both llamas and guanacos, although many times the press labelled them all llamas. Guanacos are the wild version of llamas and all have a fawn brown coat, not the variable browns, whites and blacks of the domesticated llama. I did not realise, or remember, that the

Elephant Fund was not the only fundraising campaign launched by the Zoo. In 1972 there was an appeal for £250 to fund the purchase of a mate for Panji, the guanaco. He had been at the Zoo since 1969 and from his behaviour it was recognised that he was lonely. He walked in a constant pattern about the enclosure. To help alleviate the boredom goats were introduced into the enclosure and although they helped, nothing short of another guanaco would do. An appeal saw the people of

Now for a name!

'Hi, kids,

THE Panji Fund is closed and you have raised £282.85. That's an awful lot of money and I really appreciate the hard work that has gone into raising it I haven't heard of any more fund-raising events being organised and since we have all the money we need, please don't arrange anything else. But if plans are already in the pipeline, go ahead.

Watch out next week for the short list of names my wife and I have chosen from your suggestions. We want YOU to vote for the most suitable one.

Now that school is closed for the summer my wife and I are looking forward to seeing more of you at the Zoo, especially if you bring those potato crisps that we both love!

Love, Panji'

The Panji Fund

LAST WEEK'S TOTAL—£259.30

THIS WEEK'S DONATIONS:
1st Rothienorman Cub Scout Pack £19
Susan Mitchell and Fiona Proctor,
  Bucksburn, Aberdeen 70p
"Two Patagonians" £2
Fyvie Pre-school Playgroup £1.45
Alastair Donnelly, Banff 25p
Mhairi MacRae, Muirbuie 15p

TOTAL—£282.85

Target £250

Here are Panji and his mate. Have you thought of a name for the mate yet?

120

Llama and Guanaco

the North East put their hands in their pockets and Tanji was bought from Whipsnade Zoo. The arrangements to get the animal to Aberdeen did not go to the original plan as the crate was too big to go into the train and my father ended up hiring a van and driving down to collect the young female from Whipsnade.

The fundraising appeal was featured extensively in Aberdeen Journals Junior Corner Club and in July 1972 the target of £250 was exceeded by some £32.

The pairing of Panji and Tanji was an obvious success as Jiji was born.

The youngsters' interest was kept alive by running 'name the young guanaco' competitions in the Junior Corner Club and eventually Jiji was named by the Murray family from Invergordon.

Herbert, the Llama, first footing with Dad

Monkeys

Because of the expertise available at the Zoo my father and the staff were called upon to assist in many animal matters in the local area, totally outwith the remit of the Zoo.

In 1969 a rhesus monkey escaped from the University of Aberdeen's Animal Department at Foresterhill. My father and Hugh Kay, the vet, were called upon to assist with the capture of the primate. Myrtle, the rhesus monkey, had not been used in any experiments, but her bid for freedom was far from ideal as she was likely to starve to death without access to fruit. If she had been hungry, she may have tried to steal fruit from anyone passing by. Hugh Kay tried to use a dart gun to anaesthetise her, but the range was too great as she swung about in the tops of the trees in Cornhill Road. The gun, a Kaptur tranquilising dart pistol, was purchased from the United States. I remember at the time the huge rigmarole required to import the gun. The licensing of firearms was a bit more relaxed at that time, and I remember comments being made that it would have been easier to import a

122

standard firearm which would have been far more deadly. Myrtle's 24 hours of freedom ended when my father had to shoot her, an outcome that no one wanted.

Otters

My father, like most men, liked to show off especially if his audience consisted mainly of young ladies. Picture the scene if you will. He was showing a group of trainee teachers round the Zoo. Once they reached the indoor enclosure which housed the Oriental short-clawed otters, Koko and Ovaltine recognised my father and came over to the front of the enclosure. My father opened the door and the otters came out. Now these otters are about two thirds the size of the otters we see round our coasts and rivers, and could be described as cute. The otters rolled over as my father scratched and tickled them. He had just finished explaining that otters have a bit of a reputation for biting, after all they can bite through fish, but these two were just playful. At this point the two otters decided to be less than cooperative and proceeded to shred his fingers. With blood dripping from his digits he managed to get Koko and Ovaltine back into the cage. Excusing himself he made his way back to the house. After having his hands bandaged, and forever the professional, he returned to the group of trainee teachers and continued their tour even though he was a bit embarrassed. What do they say about working with children and animals? It's difficult to avoid animals when you run a Zoo!

Pyrenean Mountain Dog

Many of the people who visited Aberdeen Zoo back in the 60s and early 70s will remember the huge white Pyrenean Mountain dog that used to park herself near the entrance.

Bergerie Javita, or Bergie as she was called, was a great placid lump of a dog who would allow children to climb all over her without so much as a bark. Only once did I see her snap her huge jaws in a show of discontent at one young child who was being downright nasty to her. The jaws made a loud clump, but they were nowhere near the little boy. However, it had the desired effect.

Although a loveable lump she was untameable. One of the staff, who had been a police dog handler, tried in vain to get her to obey commands but, to no avail; she was not to be tamed. She was not a bad dog; she just did what she wanted.

Bergie was a contented dog and I remember one winter we had a huge fall of snow and some animals, which were wintered over at the other side of Hazlehead, had to have some fodder delivered. The snow was particularly deep and we had to borrow a tractor and trailer to make the journey. Rather than sit on the trailer with us, Bergie accompanied us on foot, galloping along in the snow. I could swear she was smiling.

As Bergie aged she would sit in the staff area in the Exhibition House close to the electric fire to heat her old joints. Sometimes as she moved away from the fire part of her fur resembled griddled halloumi cheese. Eventually age caught up with her and one day she just collapsed and died.

Roe Deer

Roe deer look sweet and gentle, but my recollection is that they hide a darker side. When mucking out their enclosure the bucks would come up to you and rub their velvet-covered antlers against your shins. Normally no problem, however once the velvet was off a set of knobbly sharp

points was exposed. That in itself was not the point, no pun intended. It was the fact that the frisky male was now in rut and saw you as a rival and legitimate target. The buck would take a running charge, rearing up on its hind legs; the better to skewer parts of your anatomy. I and the other keepers had to become quite adept at parrying the little blighters' attacks utilising a brush or rake handle. Failing to position the brush shaft between the set of antlers led to a rather painful result for you, not the deer.

Although this sounds a bit risky, I remember Mikkel Utsi, the man who brought reindeer to the Cairngorms, telling how, when confronted with a charging reindeer bull, he would use a long-handled staff with a Y shape at the top. As the bull reared up on its hind legs to deliver its challenge, he would stick the end of the shaft into the ground and catch the animal's throat in the Y and, using its forward momentum, lift it off the ground. Once it was half choked, it could be let down. Given the size of a reindeer compared to a roe deer, this was risky with zero room for error.

Mikkel Utsi with Dad & the Reindeer

Vietnamese Pot-Bellied Pigs

It is hard to believe that people used to keep these pot-bellied porkers as pets. However, they can be rather cute and the Zoo had three of them: Ho, Chi and Minh. When I look back at the pictures of Minh when she was pregnant, I cannot help but think it must not have been pleasant to have a belly that, even normally, barely cleared the ground! It was reported that, as these pigs reached maturity much earlier than other breeds, many of the local pig farmers showed a considerable interest in how they developed.

Wallabies

The Bennett's wallabies at the Zoo were sourced from Mr Spence in Fife, where he had a collection of animals. I remember going down to meet Mr Spence with my father, and to see his collection. The highlight for me was going into the enclosure where he kept his cheetah! Mr Spence eventually left Fife and took up a post with Perth Zoo in Australia.

Wallabies were another of the species with which the Zoo had breeding success. In 1971 a group of children named the new arrival Rolf.

Part Three - George Leslie's Animals

In the introduction I indicated I had included eight 'chapters' which my father had written. I have named them George Leslie's Animals and have left them with a minimum amount of editing. I would ask you take into consideration that these sections were typed in the 1970s and lay unread until I started my research in 2016.

Wildcats

Oriental short-clawed otters, chimpanzees, gibbons and pig-tailed macaques are all what we might classify as exotic animals. The kind that people expect to see in a zoo along with such creatures as lions, bears and reptiles. Indeed, they could be termed as the box-office attractions. But the policy of Aberdeen Zoo, in line with trends in most modern zoos, was not simply to entertain the public, but also to instruct them. In addition, zoos should play their own part in the conservation of wildlife.

It was partly with these aims in mind that the Zoological Society decided to devote part of the Zoo to a 'Scottish Corner'. Some people, in fact, thought that the whole Zoo ought to be devoted to our native animals. The idea had a lot to commend it, but it was felt that the Scottish animals by themselves would not prove a sufficient attraction to keep people coming back, providing funds for the continued upkeep of the collection. They might, it was reasoned, come once to see such animals, but it would be the exotic animals, like the monkeys who play to an audience, that would keep them returning again and again. A happy balance was achieved between the exotic and the indigenous animals which were represented with wildcats, foxes, deer, otters, seals, pine martens, grey squirrels, birds, boars and wolves (the latter two, although extinct in Scotland, used to run wild in the countryside).

Not long before the Zoo opened, the Zoological Society got their first wildcat – MacTiddles. He came from Edinburgh Zoo and was soon ensconced in a large enclosure at Aberdeen. The enclosure was thick with long grass, trees and bushes, an ideal lair for MacTiddles, although it did make it rather difficult for the public to see him. And when they did catch a glimpse of him curled up in the long grass, fast asleep, with a peaceful, almost benign expression on his face, there were those heard to remark in a tone of disgust, *'What's so special about him? That animal looks about as wild as the cat next door'*. Before they dismiss MacTiddles and his ilk as the arch frauds of the animal world, they should look again. They should have observed his yellowish-grey fur with its narrow dark brown striping and his tail with strongly marked concentric rings. These are all ideal camouflage for the predatory life he

leads in his natural environment of the Scottish moors and mountains.

They should have looked at his dark paws, sheathing long, wicked claws – far more deadly than those of the domestic cat. They should have noted his legs – longer than those of the domestic species, designed for speed in tracking down equally fleet-footed prey such as the rabbit and mountain hare. If they were still in doubt as to the wildcat's ferocity, they should have tried going in beside MacTiddles. Or perhaps on second thoughts, that wouldn't have been a wise thing to do, for it's not for nothing that its clan has earned itself the reputation of being 'the most ferocious and cunning of British predators'.

The fact is, as I well understand, you never know where you are with a wildcat. Sometimes MacTiddles would eat out of my hand. More often than not, he would turn and spit. For wildcats will tolerate human beings, just, and no more. It is impossible to tame them.

Where the general public make a mistake is in confusing the wildcat with the domestic species. They may look vaguely alike, but in fact they are completely different. Many people assume too that the wildcat is simply an off-shoot of the domestic species gone wild, whereas in actual fact the wild and domestic cat are two separate species.

Many legends have grown up about the wildcat. These emphasise its savagery, such as it being a distinct and separate species from the domestic cat and will never mate with one, or if it does, will return at the earliest opportunity to kill the half-breed kittens. This it is true has happened, as many gamekeepers will affirm, but it is certainly not the whole story, as I discovered to my amazement.

A couple of years after MacTiddles had settled in, I received a phone call from a vet at Laurencekirk with an exciting tale to tell. He had been up at Glen Esk visiting a croft when the lady of the house asked his advice about a couple of wildcat kittens. She had found them only a matter of days old in a rock den in the glen and taken them home. There she had tried to hand-tame them without success. Even at that tender age they were wild. What was she going to do? Could she donate them to the Zoo? Of course we said yes, and arranged to go down to Laurencekirk to pick them up from the vet who had arranged to keep them for only one night. I went down, collected the animals in a trapping cage and brought them back to the Zoo where they were given injections against feline enteritis. This proved a difficult task, as the youngsters snarled and spat ferociously, and the only way to avoid injury was to ensure my hands were well protected by very thick leather gloves. Even so at the second injection one of the kittens succeeded in biting one of the keepers right through the hand in spite of the leather gloves.

As soon as possible they were liberated into the enclosure beside MacTiddles who

WILDCATS RECEIVE A JAB

These unusual photographs of a Scottish wildcat were taken in Aberdeen's zoological gardens by Ian Burns, Wellcome veterinary representative in the Highlands.

The mother cat, shown here, was injected with Burroughs Wellcome Fiovax TC as a protection against infectious enteritis, as was her litter of three.

Ian had the valued help of the zoo's resident veterinary surgeon, zoo superintendent Mr G. Leslie and his staff in obtaining the pictures accepted them both at once. In fact, they got along better with him than they had with any human contacts. To try and tame them just a little, I would go up every evening to the enclosure and stand with my back to the netting, as though paying no attention to them. Then I would start speaking as though to myself, all the time holding my hands against the netting, pushing through titbits of dead day-old chicks. Eventually I could sense the cats coming closer and closer until at last, I could feel them taking the snacks out of my hand. After that I could go into the enclosure beside them.

As the female of the litter grew older, MacTiddles took an interest in her and, indeed became so possessive that he wouldn't allow her brother anywhere near her. At last she and MacTiddles were seen to mate and in due course she gave birth to a litter –

the most peculiar litter you ever saw. It confounded the widely-held view that wildcats never mate with domestic cats, or if they do, they kill the offspring of such a match.

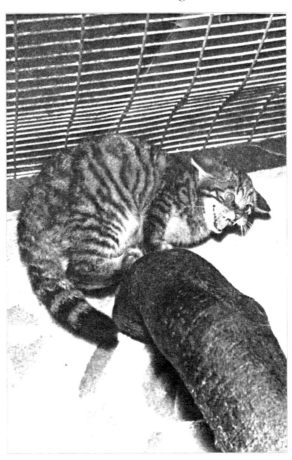

The first kitten was just like a wildcat in appearance, the second was much lighter and the third was black. Astonished staff began to wonder about their ancestry. Now MacTiddles was most definitely a true wildcat, but what of the mother, the little female from Glen Esk? The only reasonable explanation that could be found was that the female had domestic blood in her and the little black kitten was a clear throw-back to the time when the two species had intermingled. So clearly wildcats do mate with domestic cats.

As for killing their offspring, in this particular case this was also disproved, for far from MacTiddles turning on his black son, he proved a doting father to all three kittens and also a few weeks later to three adopted members of the family.

The three new kittens came from Pitlochry. They were about a fortnight old and their eyes were just opening when they arrived. Clearly, they still needed a mother, but would the female at the Zoo take them as her own? We prepared to find out. I took the three little ones and rubbed them with straw from the wildcat's enclosure. I left them at the corner of the enclosure. A short while later I was delighted to find that she had taken the three to her lair to join her true family. Their familiar smell, albeit falsely come by, established them as members of the family.

The clan was later joined by another male who arrived at the zoo in a piteous state, his hind leg having been caught in a gin trap.

Wildcats, because of their ferocity, were marked animals in Scotland; the attitude of most gamekeepers being that the only good wildcat is a dead wildcat. It is true that they wreak havoc on the grouse moors, killing off game birds. One method of hunting them, now illegal, although still in use, is the gin trap. Cruel testament to that is the mangled state of the leg of the cat brought in to the Zoo.

Foxes

Another animal hunted in Scotland because of the damage it does to lambs, poultry and other domestic animals is the fox and members of that species too have found sanctuary at Aberdeen Zoo. Among them was Foxie.

Indeed, when Foxie arrived at the Zoo, it was difficult to believe that he came from a species so hated for its killer instincts. He was as tame as a lamb, having been hand-reared by Mrs D.G. Strachan, of Millburn, Rothienorman. It may be impossible to make a pet of a wildcat but foxes, especially when young, respond to human kindness.

Foxie had been orphaned early in life (he was only a week old) when a gamekeeper in the Cabrach killed his mother for the then 10/- bounty paid for every tail, or brush. There was a half-dozen cubs left and Mrs Strachan was able to buy Foxie for £1.

At first, he was fed with a dried milk mixture from a bottle until he was old enough to eat solid food. In fact, he turned out to be no trouble at all to feed, eating everything the family had from meat to chocolate with only one exception, potatoes,

Foxie

at which he turned up his little nose disdainfully.

He lived in the garden and for recreation he had innumerable diversions. The neighbourhood children would play with him and take him for walks – just as they would a dog. Mrs Strachan even got a little white kitten to keep him company.

Unhappily he escaped from the garden one day and set off to explore a neighbour's poultry house. Although he didn't as such touch the hens, this was a signal to Mrs Strachan that he was growing up – that one day he would revert to his wild state. As she was out at work during the day and there was no one to look after him all the time, she decided, reluctantly, to donate him to the Zoo.

It was a sad loss for her, but a happy gain for the Zoo where Foxie settled in admirably - as endearing and friendly as ever.

Red Deer

One of the oldest established members of the Scottish collection was Chou Chou, the red deer hind. She came into the Zoo Society's care way back in summer 1964, a battered little orphan who, thanks to expert nourishing, survived to become a beautiful example of her species and a proud mother several times over. The baby was found with an injured neck on June 14 near Inverey by Braemar. She had been attacked by a fox, but fortunately her injuries were only superficial and after on-the-spot first aid, she was taken into Aberdeen that same evening.

The vet who examined her gave her an injection of penicillin and estimated her age, from the condition of her navel, to be 10 days. As the mother deer suckles its young for nine months after birth, a substitute milk had to be found for the orphan. Half a pint of cow's milk five times a day was suggested by the vet. Dr Lil de Kock, our honorary Secretary, took Chou Chou home to her garden and set about the programme of hand rearing. As she later recalled, '*Feeding on the first day proved very difficult*'. Chou Chou refused any size of teat. In the afternoon, however, she began drinking out of a bowl. The milk was enriched by a nob of butter, after being heated.

During the first few days some sugar was added to the warmed milk, but this resulted in diarrhoea. That was scarcely surprising, in view of the fact that analysis of deer's milk has revealed that it has nearly double the fat and protein in content of cow's milk – but less sugar. And so the sweetener was omitted from the deer's diet. For the first three weeks she was kept in a fenced paddock, but after that she was allowed the run of the garden. She chose a bare patch of ground in the rockery as a sleeping site. A comfortable place to sleep was of prime importance to Chou Chou who spent 95% of her time with her head down. The remaining 5% was devoted to eating and exploring her new surroundings. She soon started to sniff inquisitively at the garden's shrubs and not long after started to investigate their properties as food with an attempt to bite the tops off a tall heather bush. Gradually, during her second month with Lil, she began to drink more milk. The butter was now omitted, but the pure cow's milk still had to be heated to a fairly high temperature to be acceptable. This was proved definitively one day when unheated milk was offered to Chou Chou. She did take it, but began to shiver uncontrollably afterwards.

Most of the daytime was still spent resting in her chosen corner, but in the evening, Chou Chou would become adventurous, suddenly storming in colossal bounds around the garden. She also began to explore the vegetation more thoroughly. Although she still didn't eat much in the way of solids, and was as yet unable to tear off flowers and leaves, she enjoyed sucking them. Her favourites were roses, as well as the seed heads of shepherd's purse. She was also partial to decorative grasses. If any of the titbits did come away in her mouth while she was sucking them, she chewed and swallowed them.

During all this time she was becoming very attached to Lil. Gradually she forgot about her own mother (whom she had constantly called for in the first few days of her captivity) and became fixated on Lil instead. If Lil left her suddenly, Chou Chou would call after her, or if she were given any encouragement to follow, she didn't need a second invitation. Off she would go, running in leaps and bounds. She knew Lil by voice, smell and appearance, so that even if someone else put on the doctor's coat to feed her, she was not deceived. Indeed, one day, when Lil was absent, she refused milk completely. However, apart from not letting other people feed her, Chou Chou proved very affectionate to the human race in general and especially towards children, whom she allowed to stroke her dappled hide. But as Chou Chou grew older, losing the white-spotted coat of her babyhood, Lil became concerned about keeping her in the garden out of contact with her own kind. It came as a tremendous relief when she received a letter that autumn from a lady in Grantown-on-Spey offering a young male stag to the Zoo. '*I am highly delighted with your offer to donate your tame stag calf*', Lil replied. '*He will be a wonderful partner for Chou Chou who is of the same age and is absolutely tame, wandering in and out of the house…I am looking forward to meeting you and of course can hardly wait to see the calf. What is his name, I wonder?*'

His name was Phut and although it did not turn out to be quite the partner for Chou Chou that Lil envisaged, he certainly was a character. He had a very definite mind of his own, which became apparent almost as soon as he arrived. A paddock enclosed by polythene and netting had been set up in Lil's garden for the pair. But as soon as Phut was introduced to Chou Chou, he went into a panic. He rushed round throwing himself against the netting of the enclosure as though he had been put in beside an alien creature from another planet, not one of his own kind. After a while he calmed down, but not for long. Only two days after his arrival, he found a way out of the paddock and, while no one was looking, made his escape.

It was a surprising sight for the housewives of a neat suburban road on the outskirts of Aberdeen as they settled to their morning chores. No wonder they blinked their eyes in amazement, not quite sure whether to believe what they saw. For prancing down the road was the six-month-old buck on his tour of the city. But his exploration was cut short. The police were called and they soon had him cornered in a back garden, where he waited in a surprisingly docile mood until transport came to take him back to Lil's garden. '*All he had gone for was to find some children to give him*

Phut

sweets', Lil explained. In his first home in Grantown-on-Spey, Phut had apparently been used to trotting down to the nearby housing estate for titbits from the children. *'But instead of getting company and sweets in Aberdeen he was arrested'*, she added ruefully.

After this episode it was decided that perhaps Lil's garden wasn't the most suitable place to keep Phut. To prevent further escapades, he was taken to the Aberdeen Dog and Cat Home and kept in a grass paddock there. Lil was still anxious that he and Chou Chou should become companions, so she took the hind along to the Home too. Not long afterwards, she was able to report, *'They are much better friends now and are quite happy where they are. I visit them every day and the staff are very good to them'*. But she was still trying to find them a more permanent home until the Zoo opened. Eventually, the owner of a small estate on the outskirts of Aberdeen kindly put some of his land at the Society's disposal and, with the help of the Rotary Club, paddocks were erected. Phut and Chou Chou were moved in. By Christmas 1965 Phut was developing into a fine animal, already splendid in his first pair of antlers. Unfortunately, he was to learn too well how to use them!

By the summer of 1966, when the Zoo opened, the deer collection had risen to four with the arrival of Bambi and Julie. Bambi was a hind who had been raised by bottle feeding at a remote farm at the foot of Morven Hill by Mr and Mrs Robert McLaren. The deer used to bed down in a stall in the farm byre, but it was felt that a more permanent home was needed. Inspector John Taylor of the Aberdeen Association for the Prevention of Cruelty to Animals was contacted. He in turn got in contact with the Zoo who were delighted to offer the animal a home.

Julie, despite the name, was a male and Chou Chou's and Phut's first born.

In the newly-opened Zoo, the area set apart for the deer was open, not fenced in. This was alright for Chou Chou, Julie and Bambi, who mixed happily among the visitors, but it certainly could not do in the case of Phut who was proving more and more irascible and untrustworthy as he grew older. Even getting him from the paddock outside Aberdeen into the Zoo was in itself a problem. When we arrived at the paddock, we found Phut outside the fenced-in part of the field. The first thing to do, we reckoned, was to get him back inside the paddock, as it would be easier to catch him in an enclosed space. To tempt him in, I and my son Robert climbed over the eight-foot-high fence, then Robert went to open the gate and I stood in the paddock shouting for Phut. When the animal came charging in, I climbed back over the fence and Robert nipped out of the gate shutting it securely behind him. Then I, and this time Dennis the Head Keeper, ventured into the paddock again and managed to get a long rope around Phut's antlers. We held it at one end, while fellow helpers, sitting on top of the paddock's corner posts, grasped the other end. Unfortunately, those on top of the posts had given Phut too long a lead and, taking advantage of this, he immediately turned in a semi-circle round Dennis in the enclosure, his eyes bloodshot and gleaming, his teeth grinding, ready to attack.

To this day we don't know whether Dennis climbed or leapt over the eight-foot-high fence. It all happened so quickly. One moment Dennis was standing in the path of the angry stag, the next he was over that fence like a bird in flight, taking a good while to recover afterwards. I continued to hold on to the rope, while those on top managed to shorten their length, and at last they succeeded in getting Phut subdued and strapped on to a three-barred gate. With cotton wool and sticking plasters over the stag's eyes, they transported him to the Zoo, where he was put into the stable at the Children's Corner, while strong, high fences were put around the deer enclosure. In a miraculous three days the enclosure was fenced into two paddocks, one for the hinds, and the other for Phut. But it was one thing getting Phut into the stable and quite another proposition getting him from there up the length of the Zoo into the new enclosure. The stable in which he was being kept had been barricaded with lengths of wood to keep him securely in place. As soon as the wood was removed, Phut charged out with the speed of a gigantic greyhound out of trap three.

I had hoped to direct Phut up the path, at the same time protecting myself by means of a long wooden form which I was holding in front of myself. But I underestimated Phut's strength. The animal brought down his head, linked his antlers into the struts of the form and tossed it over his back, leaving me exposed in his path. There followed a mammoth chase round the Children's Corner with me hurriedly shinning up the wall onto the top of the Zoo shop, over the roof, down into the bushes at the other side and straight up the path in front of Phut to the free flight aviary. There I was able to block the stag briefly with a wooden bench pulled hastily out at right angles to the wall. Phut tossed the obstacle out of his way. I then leapt into the wallaby enclosure. Phut leapt into the wallaby enclosure after me. I leapt out. Then I took to my heels and ran on up into the deer enclosure, using myself as bait to lure in Phut. The stag fell for the simple trick, hook, line and sinker. No sooner had he followed me into the enclosure than the gate was shut behind him by a keeper and all 17 stone of me shinned out smartly over the fence.

In the summer of 1967, the red deer colony was yet again increased by another two arrivals, Bambi II and Rosemary from Glenbuchat Estate. The owner of the estate, Col. James Barclay Milne had died the previous year leaving as part of his estate a small herd of tame red deer. When Lord Cowdray took over the estate he decided he did not want them and so the Zoo, with the help of the estate's head keeper, Mr Webster, was able to acquire Bambi II and Rosemary. Unfortunately, Bambi II had to be put down due to a pelvic injury which the vet could do nothing about.

Rosemary, the Red Deer calf

Rosemary on the other hand, who was hand-reared by Margaret, my wife, thrived at the Zoo with Chou Chou and the original Bambi.

During several mating seasons, Phut severely battered all his females – Chou Chou to such an extent that her pelvis was broken, and her eye temporarily blinded. She was carried down to the stables and put inside with a false wall round her so that she could not turn around. After a fortnight, she was moved into the Children's Corner. Her limp gradually disappeared, and she tentatively worked her way back up to the deer enclosure. In order to safeguard the hinds, we decided to keep Phut away from them for good. Although in this way Phut was prevented from being a menace to his fellow creatures, there was still his violence towards humans which was steadily becoming worse.

I was the victim of one of his attacks one night when I was visiting him with a handful of sugar cubes, peanuts and apples. It was almost dark as I opened the safety catch of the enclosure to give Phut his titbits and a friendly scratch below his antlers. But in the half-light, I hadn't noticed that Phut had started to rub the velvet off his antlers. Each spring stags shed last year's antlers and almost immediately start to grow another pair. The new antlers, which are made of bone, start protruding from the skull covered in skin called velvet. As the summer progresses, the antlers grow and branch out, still covered by the velvet. Then just before the start of the rutting season at the end of September, the velvet begins to peel. At this stage the antlers feel tender and sensitive. A warning from one of the keepers, '*Watch out George, he's started to rub off his velvet*' came just too late, for I had already started to stroke the deer. He retaliated by charging into my stomach and chest tossing me. As Phut came for me a second time, I leapt off the ground and held onto his antlers with my legs around the animal's neck. This way I managed to escape attack from both antlers and hooves. Eventually, the keepers managed to free me, albeit a bit bruised and battered.

Phut's list of misdemeanours grew and grew. Not long after this episode he ran amok in his enclosure one lunch time, doing quite a few pounds worth of damage in a few minutes. There were a lot of people in the Zoo and there was a danger that Phut might escape and savage a visitor. I closed the upper part of the Zoo, got my rifle, went up to the deer enclosure, took careful aim and fired. The great stag fell dead to the ground. His tragedy was that he had been a hand-reared animal who had lost his respect for humans, and so was too dangerous to keep in captivity and equally, too dangerous to be released into the wild.

Porcupines - Maple and Syrup, the Houdinis of Aberdeen Zoo

Aberdeen Zoo's policy was to feed the animals well, give them plenty of room to exercise in an enclosure as close to their natural habitat as possible and then they would have no desire to leave. In our experience, an occasional badger or perhaps racoon may have strayed beyond the boundaries of the zoo, but on every occasion, come mealtime, they've been back at the perimeter fence.

Perhaps the most basic reason why the animals were content to remain at Aberdeen Zoo was that on the whole they had either been born there (or in some comparable place) or else they had been introduced to the Zoo at such a young age that they had grown up accustomed to the environment. For a zoo to catch adult wild animals and try to introduce them in to captivity is to invite trouble. This, sadly enough, was the case with Aberdeen Zoo's first two porcupines, Maple and Syrup – a pair of adults, both wild caught. With a lifetime of freedom behind them they never did manage to settle at the Zoo. Almost from the moment they arrived Dr Lil de Kock, Geoff Stevens and I had many adventures as we tried to track down those two very determined escapees.

The saga of Maple and Syrup started in an auspicious enough way before the Zoo opened. I, in my capacity as Curator of Mammals and Equipment for the Zoological

Society, got in touch with an expatriate animal lover, George Freeman, who had made his home in Alberta. He ran an organisation under the fabulous title of 'Ducks Unlimited – to increase and perpetuate the supply of ducks'. Could George Freeman arrange a Canadian exhibit for the Zoo?

He lived up to expectations. A fortnight later he replied, explaining that he'd been busy contacting various members of the Calgary Zoological Society and was pleased to say that the Society had agreed to send a pair of Canadian beavers to Aberdeen. Unfortunately, beavers didn't fit into the proposed plans for the Zoo. There just wasn't the space available, or the running water that the beavers would need. Another letter made its way across the Atlantic. Would it be possible to send porcupines instead? His motto might have been *'your wish is my command'*, for a fortnight later it was all arranged. Two adult specimens (smaller ones, he explained are rarely seen) had been caught for the Zoo.

By a series of fortuitous coincidences Air Canada was at that time about to make its inaugural flight direct to London. Several people in Calgary were invited to travel on the flight, including Doug Johnson, Manager of the Calgary Tourist Association. He also happened to be a Director of Calgary Zoo and had obligingly arranged to bring Aberdeen's porcupines with him. He flew into Aberdeen airport on a summer morning in June just before the Zoo opened. He cut a dash with his white Stetson and a string neck tie both adorned with silver mounted "stones". *'I dress like this'* he explained as Geoff and Lil drove him and the porcupines to Hazlehead, *'as an affectation which attracts attention and advertises Calgary'*.

On arrival Maple and Syrup were placed in a grassy, triangular enclosure opposite the Exhibition House. In the centre of the enclosure grew a tall spreading ash tree, which to the keepers seemed an excellent idea, for porcupines not only enjoyed eating bark, but also to scratch their claws on. I say 'seemed' a good idea, because the Zoo was soon to find that tree more trouble than it was worth. Within a month of being in his new home, Maple had deserted his mate Syrup and had gone a-wandering. However, on his first escape he was recaptured after only a few days freedom, and by a thousand to one chance. Lil happened to be driving along a road just outside Aberdeen late one night when she spotted in the glare of the headlights the round prickly body of Maple waddling ahead. She stopped the car, and leaping out, managed to drop a box, which she'd grabbed from the back seat of her car, on top of Maple. The last thing she dared try was to lift Maple with her bare hands – the barbed quills of a porcupine are painful to say the least. With Maple safely under the box, she promptly sat down on top of it – just in case the porcupine should decide to move off, box and all. There she sat, late at night at the side of a deserted

road, on top of a box, which in turn was on top of a porcupine, not daring to move and wondering all the while what she was going to do. It certainly was a glad moment for her when she saw a couple out walking their dog. If the pair were astonished to see a dignified, fair-headed woman sitting on an upturned box in the middle of the night in the middle of nowhere, they were even more astonished when she greeted them with '*Would you help me box my porcupine?*'

However, they obliged. Between the three of them they managed to get the box the right way up and the lid securely closed on Maple who was immediately returned to the Zoo.

But he didn't stay there for long. In fact, he was hardly back in captivity when he was off again. How on earth was he getting out? Geoff Stevens, the Zoo Manager, had assumed that each time Maple had somehow scrambled over the fence of his enclosure, which also did duty as the perimeter fence of the Zoo. But how? Then Eureka! The light dawned. It was the tree. It had seemed such a good idea that ash tree. So suitable for the porcupines. In fact, it suited too well. One of the branches stretched out towards the top of the fence. Maple hadn't needed to perform any feat of mountaineering magic to effect an exit. He'd simply had to scramble up the tree, along the branch stretched over the fence and drop to the ground. It goes without saying the offending branch was lopped off. If ever there was a case of bolting the stable door after the porcupine had fled, this was it. Still it was some consolation to think that Syrup at least was still safely inside. For the time being at any rate.

It was in December that Syrup decided to make her bid for freedom. A log rolled up against the perimeter fence by some unknown person provided her with an opportune exit. Thanks to widespread publicity in the local press concerning the escape of the two porcupines, I had many a sleepless night during my first winter as Zoo Manager. The phone rang incessantly, usually in the small hours of the morning, with people the length and breadth of the North East calling to announce that they'd seen one or other of the ubiquitous porcupines.

Dutifully I followed up all the leads, but to no avail. Until one morning in early January there came a message from the Head Forester on an estate by Aberdeen. The forester, it transpired, had been a bit perturbed by a clump of interwoven bracken he'd come across in the woods and which seemed to grow steadily every day. Could this be a nest, he'd wondered to himself? A porcupine's nest? We went out to investigate.

There in a young plantation of trees, I saw for myself the bracken mound. It was indeed a nest, a most beautifully constructed one at that. Some five-foot high by three-foot long and seven-foot broad. The bracken covering had been so cunningly intertwined that although it was pouring with rain, when we lifted the thatch, the ground beneath was perfectly dry. At the bottom lay a little platform of bracken beneath which the soil had been excavated and lined with pebbles for drainage. Entrance and exit tunnels ran from the platform angled at 90 degrees to forestall any would-be assailants. Yes, it was a nest. That had already been agreed upon. But was it Syrup's? Was she expecting young? Those questions, alas, had to remain unanswered for the time being. For despite a careful watch kept on the nest, neither Syrup, nor any other animal ever returned.

January passed, and February. A vet along Deeside found Maple so we collected him and brought him back to the Zoo, where it was noted with delight that the errant porcupine looked exceedingly healthy, more so than prior to his escape. The diet of the local countryside – birch and spruce bark, corn after harvest and acorns in the autumn - seemed to have been just what the vet ordered. But still there was no sign of Syrup. By now I was beginning to think of giving up my job as Zoo

Manager to become a night watchman instead. After all I wasn't far off being one already – what with being called out of bed night after night to no avail.

When the phone rang at 3.30 am one Monday morning in March, I blearily answered it as I had done all the others. But this one was different. This one was official. It

was from the City Police. Syrup had been 'treed' in the outskirts of Aberdeen and was awaiting capture.

Syrup, the police explained to me, had been run to earth by a taxi driver. He'd been on his way home when he'd spotted the porcupine; and leaving his car he'd followed Syrup until she'd taken refuge in a tree. Returning to his car he had contacted the police on his taxi radio, before taking up his position as sentinel at the foot of Syrup's tree. But neither the police nor the taxi driver had been able to get Syrup down from the tree, so they'd be greatly relieved if we could come out. Armed with my catching net, I quickly arrived on the scene. Sure enough, there caught up in the beam of the torch lights, Syrup sat aloft looking for the entire world like a crow's nest, while down below the police stood helplessly. There was nothing for it, I would have to go up after the porcupine.

Syrup's chosen refuge was a birch tree, not the most ideal structure to take my 17-odd stone, but up I went. The tree bent and swayed ominously as I did so. Higher and higher I climbed with my torch clenched between my teeth wondering all the while, that if the porcupine and I fell, which would be worse – landing on the hard earth, or on Syrup's quills!

Somehow – although to this day I have no recollection of how I managed it – I climbed higher than the porcupine, and then slowly tried to edge her to the ground. Some 12 feet away from my goal, I looked down aghast to see Syrup calmly waddle along a side branch and onto another tree.

What followed was a scene from Tarzan and the apes, with myself billed as Tarzan. I leapt for the other tree, grabbed hold of it, still higher than Syrup. Sensing defeat and realising it was time to admit to being beaten, she allowed herself to be edged down the tree to the ground, and into the catching net.

It would be nice if the saga of Maple and Syrup had a happy ending. But tragically it doesn't. Syrup (who had been expecting) escaped again, while still pregnant. Not long after Maple died. Romantic, perhaps to think that he passed away from a broken heart, mourning the loss of his true love, but completely untrue. Instead a long-standing liver infection, hitherto undetected, brought him to his end.

Syrup plus young are, as far as anyone knows, alive and well and still roaming the North East. So, if anyone sees a porcupine……

Koko and Ovaltine

In July 1967, Aberdeen Zoo was in the news. A rare and exciting event had taken place which thrust not only the Zoo but also two of its inmates, Oriental short-clawed otters, Koko and Ovaltine, into the limelight. The event? The birth of the otter's first cubs. Of course, the birth of any creature is a cue for celebration, but what made this birth extra special was the fact that this was the first short-clawed otter to have been born in captivity outwith the animal's native habitat of South East Asia.

Even more amazing, five-year-old father Koko had been fixated on human beings before he came to the Zoo. When he did arrive and a wife was found for him in the shape of Ovaltine, it was thought highly doubtful whether he would recognise a female otter, far less set up home and mate with one. Koko's fixation originally centred on Captain Frank Clark of the RAF's Air Reconnaissance Intelligence Unit, whose devoted pet he had been since a cub. To trace the story of their friendship, as touching as any recorded between animal and man, we have to travel back in time to over five years before the Zoo opened, when the Captain was stationed in Malaya. A keen animal enthusiast, he not only took great interest in studying the wildlife of the country, but also distinguished himself by finding a rare hornbill which went to West Berlin Zoo. He also found Koko. Koko had been captured in a fish trap in the paddy fields whilst the fields were being flooded.

Koko was put into an orange box and taken to the local market where by pure coincidence Frank happened to be wandering at the time. '*I recognised the otter as belonging to the short-clawed species,*' Frank recalls '*and was so taken by the little chap that I spent an hour trying to buy him*'.

The owner was loath to sell. '*He said,*' explained the Captain, '*that he could get a better price at the local shop where the otter would be killed and its flesh dried and used for Chinese medicine.*'

In the end a deal was made, and the owner agreed to sell the otter. Frank took the cub home where Mrs Clark christened him Coco after the clown, for he was in fact a born clown. (It was because the Clark's Chinese servant couldn't pronounce Coco, but called him by the more staccato sound Kok'o, that the otter's name changed).

Gradually Koko began to become more than just a pet to Frank and his wife. They looked on him as one of the family. When eventually they found they could no longer keep him, the loss of Koko, even to such a sympathetic environment as Aberdeen Zoo, was a great loss to them as though he had been their child. But that was still in the future. In the meantime, all was idyllic. Everywhere Frank and his wife went, Koko went too. From Malaya back to England where it was easy to get him into the country as there were no quarantine regulations. Then from Britain to Germany where Frank was posted next. So domesticated had Koko become by this time that he rode all the way to his new home curled up in the back seat of the car and adjusted himself admirably to life in a German flat.

While in Germany Captain Clark learnt of his next posting. After a short leave in England he was to go to Cyprus, and for a number of reasons Cyprus was just not suitable for Koko. But where could he leave him? A zoo seemed the obvious place, Frank thought, and duly got in touch with all his friends in the zoo world.

By now it was the summer of 1966 and Aberdeen Zoo was opening. Dr Lil de Kock was happy to offer Captain Clark a home for Koko at the Zoo. There followed a great deal of correspondence between the two, for initially the Captain was by no means confident about placing his pet in strange – no matter how competent - hands. '*Koko*', he explained, '*had become humanised as many wild animals do. Koko had lived in close contact with us and we are sure he thought we were just other otters or maybe that he was human. This, as was certainly the case with Koko, very often compensates the animal for the loss of freedom and they are very happy. Now Koko might suffer by being parted from us and we did not really want to be parted from him…*'.

They had little choice however. When they returned to Britain in September on leave with the posting to Cyprus imminent, they decided to bring Koko up to Aberdeen and hand him over. They arrived at the Zoo with Koko in the middle of the month. Everything seemed settled. But for one snag. His enclosure wasn't quite finished. The Clarks decided to take him back to England with them until it was. However, they weren't unduly depressed. Frank had just heard that his posting to Cyprus had been put off for two to three months – time enough to see the enclosure completed and to bring Koko up once more to the Zoo. Time to enjoy a few bonus weeks of the otter's company.

All too soon December, and the time for the Cyprus posting came. Early in the month Frank brought Koko back to Aberdeen. This time it was to be for good. It was still dark when I met them off the overnight train that bleak winter morning and drove them back to the Zoo. Once comfortably settled in our living room, the Captain let Koko out of his sleeping box. The otter immediately let out a high-pitched whistle. '*He wants to go to the toilet*', Captain Clark interpreted. '*The toilet? Do you mean outside?*' I asked. '*No, I mean the toilet*', the Captain repeated.

A bewildered Zoo Manager showed him the way and watched in astonishment as

Captain Clark deposited Koko on the seat. To my amazement the otter's almost human habits brought a light touch to what was otherwise a sombre day for the Captain; a little whisky helped too. And as night fell, the Captain took leave of his friend Koko who lay curled up under the sofa fast asleep, surrounded by his playthings: a rubber bone and a ball and wrapped up in an old woollen jersey which smelt very strongly of otter.

Captain Clark had agreed that if Koko settled down at the Zoo he would stay there. However, if it was felt that he was unhappy, the Captain would apply for an import permit for Cyprus, so that despite the island's many disadvantages he could be flown out to them. '*In the past*', explained the Captain, '*we found that if Koko is not at his best, his condition shows up as follows; loss of weight (his normal weight is 7 to 8 lbs); if he spends all day under his blanket; if his coat loses its soft and silky condition*'.

But he had nothing to fear. Koko settled in at the Zoo right away.

Two strange things we noticed about him were his dislike of milk and water. He steadfastly refused to drink milk. Whether it came from cow or goat, whether it was straight or diluted, he would give it a tentative sniff, then wrinkling up his be-whiskered face, turn away from the offending liquid in disgust. Nor did he show any great liking for water. He would drink it; but he steadfastly refused to swim in it. A large pool was provided for the purpose. But the nearest he would approach it was to wash his food, racoon fashion, and to wet his claws for a morning grooming session. Thinking at first that perhaps the otter found the water too cold for his liking, we went to the extent of filling a large aquarium full of warm water and tipping Koko in. Koko's response was a shriek of rage and indignation so piercing that we hastily fished him out again, reflecting as we did that Koko was obviously the exception in his species. For along with the rest of their family the short-clawed otters are renowned for their aquatic ability.

Obviously, years of acclimatisation to human ways had deprived Koko of his species' love of water. This sadly is the case with many fixated animals. Although good pets, they are no longer 'natural' in the true sense of the word. For this reason, I was not happy about introducing Koko to a female. Captain Clark had got in touch with an old friend in Penang, Mr MacVeigh, an animal dealer, and it had been arranged that he should try to find a female short-clawed otter for the Zoo. In March, three months after Koko's arrival, he wrote to me to say that he had found 'a very likely and playful specimen.' Certainly, she sounded friendly enough from further description in his letter. '*She is allowed the run of my garden everyday*', he wrote, '*and enjoys pulling about a piece of cloth and wrestles with a young Capuchin monkey which I also allow out'*. Even so I feared that putting the two otters together might have disastrous consequences. Having been brought up with human beings would Koko recognise a female otter as one of his own kind, or would he try to kill her, as has been known in attempts to introduce fixated animals.

We were soon to find out. Towards the end of March, the female was flown from Penang to Aberdeen. After she had been rested and given a precautionary injection against hookworm, she was introduced to Koko in an enclosure 20-feet long by 10-feet wide. It was sufficiently large so that either could escape from the other if the need arose. As an added safeguard his keeper stood by at the ready in case of trouble. To their amazement instead of fighting the two otters mated at once. The female did not have a name. As she was Koko's mate it was decided to call her Ovaltine.

Not only did the two otters get on well together at first, but they also retained their affection for human beings. Now I had two shadows wherever I went. When I took lecture parties through the Zoo one of the otters' favourite tricks was to play a noisy and involved game of hide and seek between the visitors' legs. They also found it equally diverting to curl up on my feet, one on each shoe. If I shook them off to walk away, I never got very far before a cacophony of squeals proclaimed that they

were after me. Most of all they seemed to like their fur stroked and the lucky one would lie in the crook of my arm whining in delight, while the other would jump up and down at my feet in a frenzy of impatience to be likewise petted.

It came as a shock to me when I picked Ovaltine up as usual one day to stroke her and she bit my hand savagely. Otters, with their strong little teeth, can give quite a bite. If they are in real earnest, they can sever the finger of a man's hand. That bite marked a noticeable change in Ovaltine's character. From then on, she became steadily more aggressive. With good reason, for it was soon discovered that she was expecting young. A two-foot square sleeping box was prepared for her within the enclosure, while, to give her further privacy, the whole enclosure was completely shuttered off and Koko removed.

On 28th July, 1967, four months after her arrival at the Zoo, she gave birth. The two-ounce male baby, was blind and almost naked, but for the hint of pale brown fur over his pink skin. He was the first of his species to be born in captivity away from South East Asia (a year earlier a similar birth had been recorded at Kuala Lumpur Zoo).

Not long after the birth Koko was returned to the enclosure and the screens taken down. Both Press and TV arrived to record the rarity of the birth, as had the public in droves. Unfortunately, the publicity seemed to go to Ovaltine's head, for instead of keeping the baby in the safety of the nesting box, she would pick him up by the scruff of the neck, carrying him cat and kitten fashion to the edge of the enclosure, where standing on her hind legs she would sway the baby from side to side for all to admire.

That led to trouble, for Koko who was the cannier of the parents and far more interested in the baby's welfare than in publicity, spent most of his time guarding his son against the mother's bouts of self-glorification. Every time Ovaltine brought her baby out, Koko wrestled to get him out of her grip and return him to the nesting box. But as soon as his back was turned, Ovaltine had the youngster out once more. Koko was in fact by far the better of the two parents. Apart from allowing Ovaltine to suckle her young, it was he who took complete charge of the baby's welfare. From this it would suggest that male short-clawed otters do make good parents and that Koko's care of his young was quite natural. Ovaltine's attitude seems to have been far less so.

I felt that the baby's health might suffer if continued to be at the centre of this prolonged tug-of-war between mother and father. If anything, the mother's temper was growing worse. We decided to replace the screens round the otter enclosure in the hope that with no audience to play up to, Ovaltine would become a more responsible mother. At first this seemed to do the trick. Peace reigned once more in the otters' home. On 6th September the baby's eyes opened. On 18th October he ate his first solid food; a raw egg and part of an eel. After that he started to eat anything he was offered. But as his appetite increased, so did his mother's aggressiveness - and this time her viciousness was channelled towards the youngster whom she seemed intent on starving to death. Although separate food trays were put out for both mother and youngster, Ovaltine would eat both, nudging the baby out of the way and keeping him at bay with snaps of her sharp teeth every time he dared approach. By November we were forced to move the youngster into an enclosure by himself for his own protection. An infra-red light was rigged up for warmth and despite the traumatic experiences the youngster suffered with his mother, he seemed to thrive by himself. That winter on one particularly frosty night the electricity failed. The next morning, I found the otter dead. I was so disappointed. Not simply because of the cub's rarity, but because death amongst our animals moves me deeply. 'He never weeps for humans, only for animals' has been said of me.

In February 1968, only a few months later, a second male was born to Ovaltine. It survived little more than a quarter of an hour. When I went to collect the dead body from the enclosure, I noticed that it had been partly devoured.

A third baby arrived in October the same year. Again, it was a male. Ovaltine, her nature having improved none, refused to suckle it. My wife, Margaret, took the baby to the house and placed it in a lined basket on top of a storage heater in the living room. It was fed on milk from a tiny pipette 12 times a day. At first the baby seemed lively enough. For five days the living room was loud with its high-pitched squeals and then silence. It too had died. I blamed the milk. Again because of the lack of records of these otters, there is no way of knowing the exact constituency of the mother's milk. Based on our experience in hand-rearing other young animals, my wife had used a proprietary brand of baby milk and added glucose.

We began to feel we had been correct in our forebodings about introducing Koko and Ovaltine. I had almost given up hope of ever having a natural otter family at the Zoo. I hoped that if Koko and Ovaltine did have another cub, it would coincide with one of the litters of our Siamese cat, Yakima. If we introduced the cub to Yakima among her kittens, perhaps she would make a good foster mother. At any rate she couldn't do any worse than the real mother. Whether or not Yakima would have accepted an otter cub, however, is something I never did manage to find out.

Six months after the death of the third cub and two years to the month since her arrival at the Zoo, Ovaltine gave birth to a fourth male on 16th March, 1969. Ten days later on 26th March she gave birth to another. Yakima didn't have kittens at the time, so we did the best we could mindful of our past unfortunate experiences with the otters. I immediately ordered screens to be nailed up around the enclosure which were only to be removed for the purposes of putting in food and cleaning out the straw. Apart from that the otters were to be left alone, in privacy and seclusion. Three months later it was noted with delight that the young otters were not only still alive but thriving. This time Ovaltine had accepted her young and for some inexplicable reason turned into a model mum.

A happy family at play in Aberdeen Zoo—Koko and Ovaltine the short clawed otters, with their twin cubs, the first to be bred in a British zoo

The otter family - for now it could truly be called a family - were moved from their heated indoor quarters to an outdoor enclosure complete with pool and specially insulated sleeping hut. This was an experiment, for these creatures were accustomed to a warm temperature in their native South East Asia, and I had reservations about how they would thrive in Scottish weather. Still it's always better to keep animals out of doors if possible, and to our delight the cold did not seem to bother them. They accepted the Scottish climate like hardy natives, exulting in their outdoor enclosure. The only part of it they ignored was the pool. The whole family seemed to have been influenced by Koko's dislike of water, for they all gave it a wide berth. Until one day I caught them unawares. They were sitting in a brief moment of repose with their backs to me, facing the water. I leant over the fence and with a quick prod of a brush toppled them all in. A drastic measure, but one that produced results. Having braved the first shock and found the water was really nice after all, they took to the pool as their favourite play place. One game they never tired of was to slide down the embankment into the pool, swim over to the other side and out again, then back up the embankment and down, up and down, up and down…

A happy family group. To visitors a delight. To me, remembering Koko and Ovaltine's earlier marital difficulties, something of a miracle.

Grey and Common Seals

'I am a man upon the land

I am a silkie in the sea

And when I'm far awa fae hame

My dwelling is in Sule Skerry'

The ballad of the silkie – or seal - who in human form woos and wins a Norwegian maid, is but one of the many legends of seals changing into men and sometimes women. These legends form a strong theme in Gaelic, Norse, Orcadian and Shetland folklore. Certainly, to see seals close up with their large inquisitive eyes, or to hear the wailing or 'keening' of their young, which sounds uncannily like the cry of a human baby, it is not difficult to understand how such myths became part of the lore of these folks whose homes fringe the North Sea. From observing the grey seals at Aberdeen Zoo, we have formed the opinion that their human-like expressions are matched by a pretty high level of intelligence – of which they've given proof time and time again.

The Zoo's small but lively colony of grey seals was much admired by visitors. One

day a teenager, not as impressed perhaps as the rest of the crowd, decided to throw stones into the pool. Whether by accident or design, a stone hit one of the seals smack on the snout as he lazed peacefully, his head just above the water. Righteously indignant and enraged, the seal swam to the edge of the pool. With his clumsy undulating movement, he heaved himself out of the water and, grunting and snorting, headed with unerring accuracy through the crowd straight for the offender. He fortunately had the sense to run straight for the gate and out of the Zoo never to be admitted again.

The day a child fell into the seal pool at the Zoo brought out another facet of these creatures' awareness. One of the grey seals gently approached the struggling child and, swimming close to him, carefully manoeuvred the infant to the shore.

In fact, we are tempted to conclude that the seal's general level of intelligence actually exceeds that of man. More specifically those humans who visited the Zoo, and without having the common sense to read the information board, label the seals as sea lions. Seals are not exotic animals, but mammals indigenous to the seas around Britain, whereas sea lions are more exotic. Perhaps that's not quite as bad, however, as the young visitor who was heard one day to exclaim '*Look mummy, look at the otters*'.

Approximately 40% of the world's population of grey seals (estimated in 2019 at 120,000) are reckoned to inhabit the seas off Britain, the vast majority off the Scottish Coast. The remainder are concentrated in two distinct regions – firstly the west Atlantic and Newfoundland, and secondly the Baltic. With such a large population of seals indigenous to our home waters, it would be easy to assume that these animals would be no trouble to keep in the Zoo. No problem of acclimatisation or diet, one could argue. The fish they lived on at sea could just as easily be obtained for them at the Zoo, whilst there would be no need for specially heated premises; just an outdoor pool. There you are – a ready-made exhibit. Yet paradoxically these creatures from off our own coasts have proved one of the most difficult species to keep successfully within the environment of the Zoo. This is something that has been experienced not only in Aberdeen, but by zoos throughout Britain and Europe.

The reasons for the difficulty in keeping seals are numerous. Although mammals, the grey seals spend the greater proportion of their existence at sea, only coming on to land at certain seasons. Not only would it be impractical to capture a healthy adult seal and introduce it to the Zoo, it would also be ethically undesirable. It was never part of the policy of Aberdeen Zoo to take into captivity an uninjured creature accustomed to a lifetime of freedom. The only way one can procure seals is to uplift them on land shortly after birth, but only if they are orphaned or doomed to be culled. Adult seals were sometimes brought into the Zoo if they had been injured or were sick and incapable of looking after themselves.

In all these cases the zoo keeper is at a disadvantage; for he has on his hands animals that require a great deal of nursing. On the one hand, hand-rearing baby seals is fraught with problems as we'll find out further on. On the other, injured or sick adult seals are usually in a pretty bad way before they reach the Zoo and caring for them calls for a certain amount of ingenuity over and above the scant knowledge there is on restoring seals to health.

Aberdeen Zoo's success in the rearing of young seals and in the treating of sick or injured adults was noted in the International Zoo Year Book of 1970. Indeed, the story of the Zoo's seals underlines as well as any the function of Aberdeen Zoo, as a sanatorium for sick animals and a centre for the advancement of knowledge, over and above its entertainment value for visitors.

The first two pups to arrive at the Zoo were not grey seals, but common or harbour

seals. Common seals give birth in the summer as opposed to the grey seals which have their young in the autumn. The baby common seals had been found orphaned in the Wash and Mr J. Taylor of the Aberdeen Association for the Prevention of Cruelty to Animals kindly agreed to drive south and uplift them.

They arrived the night before the Zoo opened, but showed little interest in their surroundings and only survived for a few days. '*We thought at one point they were going to get better, but they deteriorated suddenly*', said Zoo Manager, Geoff Stevens. '*The trouble with some animals is that once they become sick, they lose all hope. You can't tell an animal that it's going to get better or that life is really worth living and they just die. Seals are very difficult to rear - their resistance is very low.*'

Their deaths were accelerated by their refusal to feed. The milk of the mother seal is 12 times higher in fat content than that of the domestic cow. The nearest equivalent to be found was a concentrated mixture of condensed milk and margarine containing whale oil. This substitute proved sound enough; it was the method of administering it that presented difficulties. A rubber tube was forced down each seal's throat and the mixture poured in via a funnel. As soon as the tube was whipped out, the seal simply regurgitated the milk. This same method, however, was employed successfully with another baby common seal, which was brought into the Zoo not long afterwards having been found trapped in a net at Montrose some 30 miles south of Aberdeen. This seal which was far darker than usual, seemed to have a will to live. He accepted the tube and the milk/margarine mixture pumped into his stomach. His eyes became bright, his coat grew sleek. Soon he was eating herring of his own free will and living a seemingly contented, if solitary existence in the seal pool.

When I became Manager of the Zoo, it was decided to find him some grey seal companions. Although the two species tend to keep to separate territories at sea, they seemed to mix well enough in a zoo if introduced when very young. The grey seal breeding season on Orkney was approaching and an arrangement was made with a hunter who had the culling rights on Muckle and Little Green Holm, that two seals should be spared from the selective kill and, with the blessing of the Department of Agriculture and Fisheries, be transported to Aberdeen Zoo.

At the Zoo they were put into a pool along with our common seal. As they had never had any experience of catching live fish, they took very well to the dead fish that were fed to them and soon began to know very well when mealtime came round. If the keeper wasn't exactly on time they would lurch out of the pool, their heads swivelling in all directions until they set eyes upon the keeper.

It really is like getting children to take their medicine – dosing the herring

Unfortunately, in less than a year the Zoo lost both the common and the male grey seal. The grey seal was electrocuted one day by a short circuit in a pump used to empty the pool, whilst the common seal died at the beak of a marauding great skua. The great skua is a summer visitor to Britain where it breeds in the North of Scotland and the islands. A pirate by nature, this brown bird with its hooked beak and cruel claws gets its food by hustling and pursuing lesser members of the gull family, until in panic they regurgitate the contents of their stomach which the skua then dives for. The bird has also been known to kill young herring gulls and lesser black-backed gulls.

However, one day when I found two of the Zoo's injured guillemots (which were being nursed back to health) dead and was told by onlookers that they had been savaged by 'a great black bird', I thought at first that it had been a crow.

It was only the next day when I saw the 'great black bird' swoop down over the seal enclosure that I realised it was a skua. The ensuing events happened so quickly that we were powerless to prevent them. With an almighty rush of wings, the skua dived on the unsuspecting common seal as he lay steaming in the sun at the side of his pool and with one sweep of its large curved beak it tore out the seal's eyeball.

The vet was immediately sent for and an emergency operation performed. The burst pupil was removed and the eyelids stitched up. A large pool of water was set aside in the Exhibition House where he could convalesce. But instead of improving, his condition deteriorated rapidly. Eventually the seal was in such agony that it was agreed that the most humane act would be to put him down.

The only remaining seal was not left alone for long, however. The next autumn another two arrived from Orkney, again spared from the culling season. These two, christened Rhona and Magnus, were given a great welcome by the children of the nearby primary school, Walker Dam, who had a justified pride and interest in the seals, having just adopted them. The idea had originated with their headmistress who had, she said, *'thought for a long time about adopting some zoo animals'. 'I had arranged,'* she said *'to come and pick out the one I wanted when I heard through one of the children's parents about those seals. I thought that would be ideal'.*

Her plan was that the children should each contribute one penny a week towards feeding the seals, which they would visit regularly. So successful was her scheme that several more schools 'adopted' animals – among them Boddam School, by Peterhead who helped look after Sparky, the male gibbon and Bridge of Don School who took the red deer calf, Rosemary, under their wing.

A further addition to the Zoo's seal colony was Pierre – named after Pierrepoint, the last British hangman. Unlike the others Pierre wasn't brought into the Zoo in infancy, but at the estimated age of around one and half years. Pierre had got inextricably entangled in a salmon net just south of Aberdeen. The more he writhed and twisted the deeper the thick nylon cut into his neck until at last the salmon fisherman, despairing of cutting him loose, had hauled nets and seal onshore. Knowing that Aberdeen Zoo was on the lookout for seals, he phoned to say that if I could get the seal free, it was ours.

It was March and almost dark when my wife and I arrived at Cove where the struggling seal had been beached. The fishermen were reluctant to help us free the seal, pointing out that if these animals could inflict such dreadful injuries on salmon, they were not risking the same injuries being inflicted on them.

With my hands protected by heavy gloves, I managed to free the seal, though the net was embedded so deep that we had to cut the seal's flesh to sever it. A sack was thrown over the seal and, snapping and protesting, he was heaved into the back seat of our car. His temper hadn't improved any by the time he reached the Zoo. Pierre bore the mark of that net, a thin groove encircling his neck, which was especially noticeable when lying out in the sun, and which looked for all the world like the mark of a hangman's noose.

Once at the Zoo he refused to go into the pool, he refused to eat, snapping aggressively when anyone dared come near him. After four days his condition was becoming serious. He had already lost almost one third of his body weight. If it continued the seal would be dead before long and so it was decided to start force feeding him. This was a tricky, hazardous business requiring two fairly strong and determined keepers. Wearing heavy gloves, I cautiously approached the seal from behind and straddling it, bent down and opened its jaws wide. Then one of the keepers would slide some fish down its throat. Two pounds of herring, four times a day, were fed to the seal this way until after seven days Pierre decided it was preferable to feed himself. As soon as he started feeding, he joined the others in the pool where he quickly established himself as the leader.

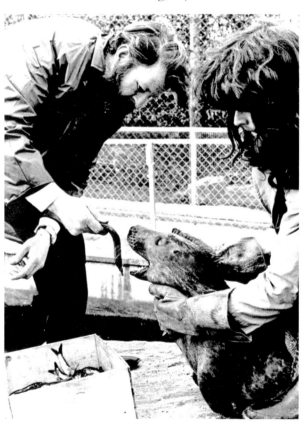

Another young seal caught in a salmon net at Cove wasn't so fortunate. Whereas the sum total of Pierre's injuries had been a cut neck, this youngster arrived at the Zoo unconscious with a cracked skull, ear damage, bleeding nose and broken teeth. These injuries had been inflicted by salmon fishers who had found the seal in their nets. When we got the seal to the Zoo, there didn't seem to be much hope for it. I placed it in the shallow pool in

Dad and John feeding Pierre

158

the Children's Corner where it lay for a day and a half, still barely conscious with only its eyes and nose above water. Because of its nose and mouth injuries it was impossible to feed it. However, it did have a will to live. Gradually, without any prompting it came round and began to swim - albeit feebly and with a curious lop-sided movement, its balance having been affected by the ear injuries. It started to feed and gradually regained its strength.

The Zoo would have liked to keep this indomitable creature, but it happened to be a bull. With two bulls already, there just wasn't room for another and so it was sent to the Bristol Wildlife Park.

Chimpanzees, Gibbons and Monkeys

If it were possible to single out one animal at Aberdeen Zoo that stood head and shoulders above all others in terms of popularity, that animal would be Humphrey, the Zoo's male chimpanzee.

It is a fact that in most zoos monkeys, and more specifically chimpanzees, are star attractions. Perhaps the reason lies more in human psychology than with the monkeys. Most human beings seem to have an innate and spontaneous preference for animals that bear the closest resemblance to themselves. The sight, for example, of a monkey drinking out of a cup which it is holding in its fingers like a human evokes some deep and pleasurable response in Homo sapiens. The way chimpanzees, especially young ones, readily respond to a human audience sets the seal on this bond of attraction.

As well as being a great favourite with visitors to the Zoo, Humphrey enjoyed equally affectionate attention from the staff who regarded him almost as the Zoo's mascot, for the day of his birth coincided as near as can be calculated with the opening of the Zoo. Consequently, 16th July was always a dual celebration of the Zoo's anniversary and Master Humphrey's birthday. It was usually celebrated with a reception held by the Zoological Society and a party for Humphrey attended by about 20 children, with Humphrey himself the guest of honour. Margaret, my wife, always prepared a fine spread of food as one would for any youngster. There were sandwiches and chocolate biscuits, buns and cream cookies and smack bang in the middle of the table an iced birthday cake with the appropriate number of candles.

To an outsider this may seem at first glance a little ridiculous. Whoever heard of anyone throwing a party for a chimpanzee? In any case, the critic might continue, this smacks of using an animal just for the sake of human enjoyment. Surely the poor monkey can't enjoy all the ridiculous paraphernalia of a birthday party with chocolate, cake and candles, but Humphrey did. He may not actually have known what a birthday meant, but had a jolly good idea what cake tasted like. It was his favourite food; whilst as far as children were concerned, he loved them and their company.

Humphrey celebrated many birthdays at the Zoo. Watching the antics of this bundle of endearing mischief, it was difficult to remember that this was the same sickly baby who arrived shivering and very ill at eight months old one morning in April in the first spring after the Zoo opened.

Humphrey was brought to the Zoo by Bob Jones, a civil engineer, who had just returned from a tour of duty in Sierra Leone. It was while he was in Africa that he had bought Humphrey from a school teacher who in turn had bought him from a hunter. An affectionate, docile animal, Humphrey had been brought back to this country by Bob Jones as an intended present for his wife. The plan however misfired and Humphrey found himself yet again changing hands. This time to Aberdeen Zoo.

When I first saw the animal, I immediately realised how ill he was. He lay, an incongruous little figure, lost in a white baby's romper suit, his wrinkled, distressed face framed in a jaunty (but in the circumstances pathetic) matching pixie hood fringed with pink. The clothes had been bought by Bob Jones immediately on landing in this country to protect Humphrey from the drastic drop in temperature after Sierra Leone. But to no avail. Humphrey had caught, and was suffering from, that commonest of all human ailments, the common cold. He was suffering badly. After all, he was only a baby, and a weak one at that, with no resistance. His large brown eyes were weak and watery, his nose stuffed with mucus. His breath came in painful gasps.

It was obvious from the first that he could not possibly be left out in the prepared enclosure in the Zoo. He needed constant care and attention. Due to the lack of a hospital unit at the Zoo, the only place where he could be looked after properly was in our house. Once in the house, we removed the chimp's pixie hood which revealed a long scar running over the top of his skull and straight down his forehead which, added to his watery eyes and stuffed nose, made him seem an even less prepossessing figure. Although unsightly, it was an old scar, almost healed, though the hair had not started to grow over it yet. Humphrey had come by it when he was captured by a hunter in Sierra Leone.

In their natural habitat chimpanzees move about in tight social groups, incorporating an older male, perhaps three younger males and up to eight females and their young. Every night they build a fresh nest in the trees. During the season the hunters arrive before dawn at the foot of the trees. They're on the lookout for young chimps, adults being difficult to transport and also being less likely to adapt to a new environment in a zoo. To capture the young chimps, the hunters shoot the females. Then, when the mother has tumbled from the tree with the baby still clutched in her arms, they pick up the young and run before the older chimps come down to pursue them. It would seem that Humphrey still bore the graze from the fall that killed his mother.

A basket was prepared for him on top of the storage heater in the living room where he lay for a week. He was so lethargic and weak, he scarcely moved, nursed all the

Mum with Humphrey

while by my wife, just as if he were a human baby. The comparison isn't as far-fetched as it seems. It was just like having a baby in the house. Feeding bottles had to be obtained for Humphrey to suck down the glucose and water mixture prepared for him. During the first week that was all he could manage. Indeed, he had to be prodded awake to get his bottle. For the rest of the time he just lay fast asleep, wheezing piteously. Mammoth piles of disposable nappies had to be bought, for Humphrey needed changing many times a day. On top of that he needed the added protection of clothes to keep him warm. Here Margaret came to his aid. A quick phone call to her sister who had a toddler, and she had Humphrey's wardrobe stocked up with dungarees, jumpers, pants and everything that her sister's child had outgrown. Enough in fact for Humphrey to have two changes of clothes a day, if necessary, and an extra load for Margaret in the weekly wash. The purchase in bulk of rubber breeks completed his outfitting.

By the third week Humphrey was beginning to sit up and take notice of his surroundings. He had graduated from glucose and water to vitamin syrup, Farex and honey. Spoonfuls of the latter, plus liberal applications of Vicks vapour rub on his chest were beginning to dispel his cold. He was starting to show, now that his health was gradually being restored, that far from being passive, he was a demanding little infant. He wholeheartedly adopted me as his protector, so much so that when it came to mealtimes, or nappy changing, he would let no one touch him but me. That was all very well, but as Manager of the Zoo I had more to do than nurse one sick chimp. Just occasionally I did get a long lie instead of being up with the early birds to change Humphrey's morning nappy.

Determined one day to have that longed-for lie-in, I decided that Margaret could see to Humphrey for a change. She was quite agreeable to the idea. Humphrey, unfortunately was not. At the sight of the approaching figure of Margaret he started to scream. Most parents are surprised at the sound of their first infant's raging. Their first reaction would have how could such a volume of ear-piercing sound emerge from the lungs of such a tiny creature. Humphrey's yells were double the decibels of any human baby. Margaret held her ground. *'Now then, Master Humph'*, she pronounced firmly, as she changed the loudly protesting chimp's nappy, *'now then that's enough from you'*. Humphrey continued to scream, but the nappies were changed and realising no doubt that there was nothing to fear in the benign figure of my wife, Humphrey promptly adopted her as his mother and Margaret had a new job. From that day on she was promoted to chief nappy changer and bottle washer to Master Humph.

After this a definite routine was established. Whereas at first Humphrey had woken up at nine or ten at night for his last feed, by now he was on to solids (his favourite being tinned rice pudding and cherry cake). After a meal at 5:00 pm he was put down to sleep on his basket on top of the storage heater. Normally he would drop right off and that would be him settled for the night, but occasionally he would wake up to catch us at our supper and immediately wail long and loud for more cherry cake. If it was not forthcoming, he would jump up and down in his basket enraged. Eventually it was decided that to give him more privacy and us more peace at night he would be moved through to a cage in the study. From then on, we could enjoy our supper in tranquillity.

During the day Humphrey was allowed out of his cage to play freely in the house and to take his meals with us. At mealtimes he would either sit on Margaret's knee or on a chair beside her, just like an ordinary member of the family, which indeed he was. By this time, he'd learnt to drink out of a cup (far quicker than any human infant), although he still preferred a bottle which he would lie and suck for hours after he had drunk it dry. It was only when Margaret discovered that he was growing strong enough to chew right through the teat and finally break the bottle itself that we took it away from him for good. As for playing, Humphrey would find endless ploys to keep himself amused. He would sit beside the Siamese cats and gently stroke them for hours, much to the pleasure of the cats. He didn't, however, hit it off quite so well with our other pet, an African grey parrot. When Humphrey put his fingers through the cage to try and stroke it, he was rewarded with a sharp peck on his fingers which put him off parrots for life. He had a variety of rubber toys, plus a set of assorted blocks to be hammered into a piece of wood with corresponding holes. After the first attempt he matched all the shapes to the holes and would sit happily banging on the blocks for hours. Another of his favourite pastimes was drawing. He was given paper and magic markers and would scribble enthusiastically for long periods of time. For some unfathomable reason, his favourite colour was orange.

Although he was allowed the relative freedom of the house all day, he never touched any ornaments, nor broke anything lying around. In fact, in the six months that he was in our house, only once did he blot his copy book. That was when we decided to take one of our few breaks from work. We set off on an overnight trip to the country leaving Robert, our son, in charge. Humphrey had been securely locked up in the study, but unbeknown to anyone he had discovered how to release the bolts. The next morning when we returned home, we found chaos. Robert had gone out and taking advantage of the empty house, Humphrey had let himself out of his cage to go in search of cherry cake. In the process he had managed to tip quite a few packets and tins out of the kitchen cupboard, but in the end he found his cherry cake. There he was sitting on the kitchen floor in a mess of butter, sugar and flour, a piece of cake in one hand and a bottle of milk in the other. If we were flabbergasted at the sight of Humphrey, then Humphrey was equally surprised to see us. So much so that he let go of the bottle of milk with a start. It smashed on the floor to add to the mess. '*I didn't know whether to laugh or cry*' my wife recalled later. She ended up laughing, fortunately for Humphrey. But at the same time, it was decided that he was becoming too big for the house and it was time he joined the other animals in the Zoo, where he belonged.

Nobody knew for sure how Humphrey would take to his enclosure at the Zoo after becoming such a well-established member of our household, and so the move was made very cautiously. At first Humphrey was taken to his new home during the day only, returning every evening to his old sleeping quarters in our house. Fears on

Humphrey's behalf proved groundless, for the arrangement suited him very well. The born extrovert was not slow to realise that this way he had the best of both worlds. He was still the centre of attention in the house, while, as an added bonus, he was finding a new circle of admirers in the Zoo.

The first social event of his day was his morning cup of milk which he always took with the keepers at their tea break. Then it was a walk round the Zoo before returning to the enclosure to show off in front of the visitors. He loved an audience. But visitors or no, he always insisted on an after-lunch nap. No matter how many people were gathered round his enclosure at that time he would refuse to be distracted from his purpose. He would slip into his cot cuddling his teddy bear (although he didn't know it, he had two teddy bears, both identical which Margaret would interchange when one needed washing), pull his blanket over his head and have his forty winks. He was still very attached to my wife. If he were out in the Zoo surrounded by a group of visitors and Margaret appeared at the back of the crowd, he would recognise her immediately, start whimpering and work his way through the crowd to be with her. But gradually, as he spent more and more time in the Zoo and out of the house, he transferred his fixation to John his keeper. This was the signal to move him full-time into the Zoo.

Humphrey excelled himself as a public relations officer. When very important visitors arrived, he was at the forefront of the reception party. When posters were needed to advertise the Zoo, it was Humphrey who was portrayed on them. When newspapers wanted photos of animals, Humphrey was selected. He was invited to children's parties and cinema shows and to appear on television. He even did a series of TV commercials for a lemonade company. The advertisement required Humphrey to walk up to a table laden with lemonade bottles of different flavours, take one, open it and drink it down. Humphrey needed no coaching to do that, for he loved lemonade and opening bottles was child's play to his nimble fingers.

At CHRISTMAS and NEW YEAR EVERYONE, yes EVERYONE asks for

Hay's SOFT DRINKS

MAKE SURE YOU HAVE ENOUGH FOR YOUR PARTIES!

WM. HAY & SONS (ABDN.) LTD. 14 BERRYDEN RD, ABERDEEN. Phone 26231

All in all, it was almost impossible to recognise the chubby, self-assured chimp before the TV cameras as the same sickly animal who had first arrived at the Zoo. Apart from the occasional cold that still afflicted him, he was a hale and hearty fellow with an appetite to match. For breakfast he would tuck into a substantial spread of baby food, bone meal, vitamin syrup, brown bread, apples and lettuce, washed down by a pint of goat's milk. For lunch it was more brown bread and currants and vegetables and for supper he had oranges, vegetables and his all-time favourite, a large slice of cherry cake. All the extra snacks that people wanted to give him had to be monitored carefully, as chimps have a tendency to overeat and become potbellied.

As Humphrey approached the age of two, concern grew over his solitary state. It did not, it would seem, bother Humphrey himself one little bit. We realised that if a chimp was kept too long on its own, it becomes so fixated on humans that eventually it becomes impossible to introduce it to another of its own species. Of course, chimps don't mate until they're about five or six years old, but to have waited until Humphrey was mature was running the danger of having him attack and possibly kill any female chimp that was brought near him. If he was introduced at the tender age of two, chances were that he would get along fine with a companion. Therefore, we started on a search for a female for Humphrey. I scanned the various dealers' price lists for a likely animal. However, such was the demand for young chimps that by the time I wrote off, the animals were invariably sold. At last I noted that a dealer in Holland had a list of chimps: one pair a year and half old, a pair three years old and a third pair six years old. It was 6.30 in the evening when I first looked at the list. By 9.30 next morning I was on the phone to Holland. The younger pair had already been sold, but the dealer said he could manage to find another young female chimp. Thinking my search was over I put down the phone.

The formalities were soon completed and word arrived that the chimp would be dispatched right away. The arrangements were that the chimp would be flown from Holland to Aberdeen. However, the plan misfired. The day that I was due to collect the chimp from Aberdeen Airport, a phone call came to say that the chimp was in Glasgow. The chimp had been there since 4:00am in the morning, so we decided to drive down right away and collect it. We loaded up the car with a plentiful supply of fruit and I set off with my son Robert in high spirits to collect Humphrey's prospective mate. At the airport, however, we were staggered to see the size of the crate the animal was in. It was enormous, considering it contained such a small chimp. I was even more surprised at the weight. It was so heavy that Robert and I only just managed to manhandle it into the back of the spacious car. But the final and worst surprise of the day came when we decided to give the animal some food. On opening up the sliding panel on the crate, we looked in a mixture of dismay and horror at the large hairy hand which was bigger than my own that slid out to grab the fruit. I looked at Robert. Robert looked at me. We decided without more ado that the best thing would be to take the crate back to Aberdeen unopened and release the 'monster' in the safe confines of the Zoo.

As soon as we got home and opened the crate, we saw that our worst fears had been realised. The chimp appeared to be far too big and too old to be a mate for Humphrey. Still we reckoned, clutching at a last straw, perhaps it was as tame as the dealer had claimed. Possibly everything would turn out alright, in spite of the unpropitious beginning. The next day the older chimp was introduced to Humphrey, who took one look, and, chattering violently, shot right up to the top of his cage, where he cowered trembling, refusing to come down. Down below Peggy, as the female had been christened, was playing nonchalantly with a three-legged stool. I leant forward to take the stool from Peggy, intending to put it down on its legs so that she could sit on it. Still appearing quite friendly and relaxed, she stretched forward, took hold of my fingers, and apparently playfully and calmly gripped them in her mouth. When I at last managed to extract them from her vice-like jaws, the whole hand was swollen, while one of the fingers was minus a nail. She then went back to playing with the stool. Such a callous creature was not going to prove a very satisfactory companion for Humphrey. It was a shaking but very relieved male chimp that watched Peggy being cajoled out of his cage a few moments later by the keepers, and taken back into the lecture theatre to another cage.

The next day the dealer in Holland was notified that the chimp failed to come up to expectations and, unless she showed any signs of improving in the next few days, she would be sent back. Instead of improving, she became worse. A few nights later she escaped from her cage in the lecture theatre and cornered John who had been assigned to look after her. He tried to reach the internal phone to get in touch with me, but Peggy kept him cornered and it was a heart-stopping hour before he was able to escape. Peggy had set the seal on her own destiny. The verdict was that she could not be trusted and, so without any more delay, she was sent back to Holland.

I was becoming more and more frustrated in my attempts to find a suitable companion for Humphrey, but I continued to try and at last our perseverance was rewarded when a phone call to a dealer in England brought welcome news that his firm had a hand-reared female chimp, between one and two years of age. The chimp had been orphaned in Nigeria and hand-reared by a school teacher in the country.

The animal was still in Africa, but if we gave the word…

I did. And the creature was duly dispatched to Aberdeen where Heather, as she was christened, proved to be just what we had been looking for. For a few days she was kept by herself so that tests could be carried out to see if she was free from worm. After getting a clean bill of health, she was introduced to Humphrey. They took to one another right away. It was a few days before Humphrey's birthday and it seemed, as far as we were concerned, that he couldn't have got a better present.

Although Heather had known human company in Nigeria, she wasn't quite as tame as Humphrey, a fact that became increasingly clear when it came to trying to put a collar on her. Humphrey accepted this as a matter of course when he went out for walks, but not his companion. For the first three months she would not let anyone try picking her up, far less put a collar on her. Finally, she compromised and would allow John to take her by the hand. This was all very well inside the Zoo, but not the case outside. Humphrey was still getting lots of invitations to social events like tea parties, and it would have been an extra surprise for their hosts had Heather accompanied him. There was always the danger that collarless, she might become

Tea party with John and Humphrey

168

excited and uncontrollable among strangers.

One future big event was the chimp's tea party at Hazlehead Park; the Zoo's contribution to the annual Aberdeen Festival. If only Heather would accept a collar, then she could go as well. The series of tea parties in the park was due to be held in the summer just under a year since Heather's arrival at the zoo. Rehearsals started in late spring. Every day Humphrey had his collar put on and off he would go to a mock-up tea party. Of course, Heather didn't know where he was going, but she did know when he returned and food was brought to him; he was never hungry. Obviously, he was being fed on these mystery excursions. There was one thing that Heather could not resist and that was food. The idea that her mate was getting access to some supply that was denied to her was too much. This called for investigation. If it meant a collar, then too bad, a collar she would accept.

For a while after this she accompanied Humphrey on the social round. With both of them collared, John their keeper could also take them out on long walks every morning. As a special treat, he let them off their leads to swing round the trees surrounding the nearby golf course. Let off the lead, they behaved like a couple of children, swinging from branch to branch and often, for a while, ignoring their

John Buchan with Heather and Humphrey

169

keeper's commands to return. This was all very well when they were young and fairly lightweight, but as they got older it presented problems. It is difficult to handle two nine-stone chimps at the end of a leash, especially two with a tendency to gang up on the keeper for scolding one or the other. This was seen most dramatically as they were being taken back to their cage one day. Heather suddenly grabbed the fence and refused to go on. John tried to prise her loose and she nipped him. I immediately grabbed hold of her, and as I did Humphrey started to nip me. It was warning sign that the chimps were growing powerful – a pointer that if they ever did decide to lose their temper in earnest, they might be impossible to handle. In future, when they were taken out, they were put on a new lead. Each lead was made partly of chain and partly of long metal poles. The poles interlocked together, so that in the case of trouble, the chimps could be safely isolated at each end of the six-foot pole.

Their increased size also meant that they needed a larger enclosure than the little home they'd had in their babyhood. A collection box was placed outside their enclosure and the estimated £2,000 needed was trickling in steadily when a local businessman died, leaving a substantial sum to the Zoo. This enabled the Zoo to go straight ahead with the new enclosure, a sumptuous building complete with spacious play area and sleeping quarters, which provided a permanent home for the chimps.

Heather, however, nearly didn't live to enjoy her new home. One night, tragedy struck, and it was a miracle that she survived. The chimps had just moved into their new home when one night, while I was paying them my usual evening call before turning in, I heard Heather groan. Going into the sleeping quarters to investigate, I found that Heather wouldn't let me near her. I went to get hold of John and eventually managed to get the sick chimp back to my house, by taking Humphrey as well. Heather lay whimpering in agony. There was no sign of any external injury, and so the vet was sent for. Before he arrived, Heather's pupils had slid up above her eyelids, and her breathing seemed to stop. John rushed to feel her pulse. *'She's dead'*, he muttered. However, I could still feel a slight fluttering of breath against my hand. We immediately started to apply artificial respiration and Heather slowly came round. When the vet arrived, he examined Heather and decided that she had an obstruction in her gut. The only hope was that she would pass it out.

The chimps were taken back to their enclosure for the night. Their anxious keeper John spent an anxious vigil beside them, alert to any deterioration in Heather's condition. The next morning a button was found amongst her droppings. This was what had brought her nearly to death, and, as no member of the Zoo staff would have been so stupid as to have left such a potentially dangerous object lying about, it was assumed that a visitor had thoughtlessly given it to the chimp. All's well that ends well and Heather fully recovered from her ordeal. But there have been other monkeys in the Zoo who have not escaped so happily from the folly of human beings.

Two promising partnerships, one of a pair of gibbons and another of pig-tailed macaques, were all too tragically broken by the thoughtless acts of visitors.

The first casualty was a pig-tailed macaque called Bimbo, wife of Chan, both of whom were amongst the Zoo's original members. Chan had started life as the pet of a Chinese family in Borneo, where he lived as part of the household until one fateful day when his master caught him stealing food from the table. The owner reached for his cleaver, brought it down and that was the end of the fingers on Chan's right hand. Geoff Stevens, the Zoo's first Zoo Manager, who was at the time Organising Commissioner for Boy Scouts in Borneo, heard of the incident. Shocked by the treatment meted out to the monkey, he succeeded in getting him from the owner. Geoff's kind treatment did a lot to restore Chan's badly shaken faith in the world around him. When he was introduced to a mate, Bimbo, he settled down extremely well. There was only a rare flash of over-aggressiveness as a reminder of his very disturbing experience. However, those rare flashes of anger have a bearing on the story.

When they arrived at Aberdeen Zoo, all was going well for the macaque couple until almost a year after the Zoo opened. A visitor, in a rush of misdirected kindness, ignored the 'No Feeding' notices and handed Bimbo a square of chocolate. This wouldn't have been too bad had she handed a piece to Chan as well, but she didn't. To make matters worse she immediately produced a second piece and handed that to Bimbo too. All the while Chan was becoming more and more enraged. Used to being the master and, as such, being fed first, the sight of Bimbo getting not one, but two, pieces of chocolate, was too much for him. He turned on his terrified mate and shook her so violently that by the time we arrived Bimbo lay dead with a broken neck.

Tragedy number two struck the next morning. As I was touring the Zoo about 8:00am, I saw to my horror the limp body of Monk, the male gibbon. He was sprawled on the ground in the open part of the enclosure, with Mimi, his mate, standing over him pathetically, trying to lift him up into the warmth. Dashing into the enclosure I picked the ape up and carried him to the house where I laid him on the storage heater. All attempts to revive Monk failed, and in a few hours he was dead. An autopsy revealed that he had swallowed a polythene bag, causing an obstruction. Whether the lethal object had been given to the ape by accident or design, no one will ever know. The reasons behind it aren't really significant, for, whatever the intent, Monk was well and truly dead and Mimi inconsolable. So too was Chan, the macaque, at the death of his mate Bimbo. We decided to act quickly to find replacements, before they had a chance to mope for too long. A white-handed gibbon, Sparky, was found for Mimi, while two female macaques were bought from a London dealer for Chan.

Chan took to his new companions quite well. However, he had a tendency, which manifested itself every few months, of suddenly and, for no apparent reason, ill-treating them. After a while we found a solution to this. Whenever Chan got into one of his moods, we would put a collar on him and fix him by a short lead to one of the corner posts of his enclosure so that, although he could move about, he couldn't get near the females. This was enough to show him that his actions were disapproved, and eventually he gave up worrying his companions. One other precaution which had to be introduced was that the females had to be fed separately from Chan, for given half a chance he would have pinched their food. He had an enormous appetite. Green vegetables, carrots, potatoes, seeds, brown bread, biscuits, eggs, nuts… he would munch his way through a wide variety of food. In case he ever did bite off more than he could easily chew, he put the two pouches, one on each side of his mouth, to good use, as larders in which to store extra supplies. Each pouch was big enough for a hard-boiled egg, which was very convenient as these were his favourite food.

Pig-tailed macaques are found in Borneo and Malaya and are members of the same family as Rhesus Monkeys. In fact, their other name is greater rhesus. The intelligence of the rhesus is well-known, and macaques do not lag far behind when it comes to brain power. Indeed, so sharp is the macaque's ability to learn quickly, that in Borneo they were trained to shin up the coconut trees, twist off the ripe coconuts, and throw them down to the ground. Down below the most intelligent ones were known to sort the nuts out into sacks.

However, at Aberdeen Zoo, Chan started to put his intelligence to more unorthodox uses, among them collecting spectacles. This proved to be no chance affair, but a carefully worked out strategy on Chan's part. There was a gap of three-feet between the netting of the enclosure and the public. This was far too wide for Chan to be able to stretch out his hand and grab a visitor's spectacles. What the wily monkey did was to stand at the netting with his hand outstretched, offering a peanut to any passing bespectacled person. As the unsuspecting victim leant forward to accept the gift, Chan would immediately let the nut drop into no-man's land of the protection area. Predictably the visitor would lean forward to pick it up. In a flash

Chan would stretch forth his hand and another pair of spectacles landed in his collection. Needless to say, this caused us a great deal of bother - some visitors even threatened to sue. In desperation we put up a large notice beside the enclosure that said 'Beware, this animal collects spectacles'. That didn't deter the monkey from getting up to his tricks, but at least people had been warned! Unfortunately, Chan's mischievous little life was cut short, when he managed to work his way out of his enclosure one day and bit his way through a power cable, electrocuting himself. I grieved for the monkey, for all his sometimes-bad-tempered ways, he had been a delightfully friendly animal towards his keepers and a real character.

Another three females and a male, James, were bought to swell the macaque colony and Chan's erstwhile companions soon forgot their old friend and turned their attention to James.

In a short while, one of their number, Bertha, produced the troop's first-born, Sylvester. The sight of the tiny macaque – with his scraping of red and grey fur, clinging to his mother's underside fascinated visitors, as is always the case with baby animals. As he grew, he would move tentatively, his little fingers hooked into his

Bertha, the pig-tailed macaque and baby Sylvester – one of the breeding successes

mother's fur, up onto her back and from there take flying leaps onto the mesh of the enclosure. Sometimes he would make contact with the net, and then from there leap back onto his mother's back. Other times he would miss and fall in a little aggrieved heap on the ground, half bounding and half crawling after his mother. He was eventually joined by a baby half-sister and brother. The macaque family continued to breed and they become quite a sizeable troop, despite the inauspicious beginnings with Chan and Bimbo.

No such good fortune attended the gibbons, however. Mimi as you recall was given a new mate, Sparky, to replace Monk. The animals were kept for a few weeks in adjoining cages and then moved in together. To all intents and purposes, they seemed to get on well. One day, Mimi was found dead. A post-mortem was carried out, but no physical cause of death could be found. Mimi, it was sadly assumed, had died of a broken heart still pining for Monk. The unknown person who had pushed the polythene bag into the gibbons' cage had wrought far more tragedy than he or she could have realised. By this time Sparky was becoming too old to be introduced to a new companion, so he lived alone at the Zoo. What he lacked in company from fellows of his own species, he made up in human attention, for he was adopted by an Aberdeenshire school. Every week the pupils of Boddam School collected their pennies and sent them to the Zoo for Sparky's upkeep; they also came to see him as often as they could.

Great Escapes - Corporation of the City of Aberdeen - Aberdeen Zoo

Recovery of animals from outside the Zoo enclosure

Links and Parks, 18th October 1966

Day	Date	Description	Time recovered
Tuesday	23rd August	Two lambs in park	2.00 pm
Wednesday	24th August	One white rabbit in park	12.30 pm
Wednesday	24th August	Two lambs in park	1.30 pm
Wednesday	24th August	Two pheasants	10.00 am
Thursday	25th August	Two lambs on Golf Course Road for one hour	12.00 noon
Saturday	10th September	One white rabbit in park	
Monday	12th September	Two lambs in park	
Monday	12th September	One ram, two sheep from stockyard field at swings. Ram caught in garage - Woodburn Avenue. Two sheep on Hazledene Road	
Tuesday	13th September	Two lambs in park Two goats in park Two lambs in park One lamb in park One white rabbit in park	10.45 am 11.15 am 1.00 pm 1.30 pm
Friday	16th September	One golden pheasant	11.00 am
Thursday	22nd September	Two goats in park	
Tuesday	27th September	One duck	2.00 pm
Thursday	29th September	One chicken One goat	11.00 am
Thursday	29th September	Two goats in middle of dahlia bed	1.10 pm

Wednesday	5th October	One deer on Golf Course Road	5.00 pm
Wednesday	5th October	One pheasant	Out all day
Monday	10th October	Three sheep	
Thursday	13th October	One pheasant in park	8.00 am
Thursday	13th October	Three sheep out of stockyard field	10.30 am
Thursday	13th October	Three goats in park	3.00 pm
During summer, July - August		Six wild rabbits escaped	

Quite an ominous sounding document! Fifty escapes from the zoo in as many days after its opening. Add to that chipmunks being chased with butterfly nets round the GPO Sorting Office at Aberdeen Station: chinchillas at large in the boiler room at the local Music Hall: lemmings lost in the countryside: multi-coloured macaws flying free in one of the city parks and you may well wonder if there were not more Zoo inmates at large outside the Zoo than in.

If it's a sensational picture, it's also a misleading one. For Aberdeen Zoo had been remarkably fortunate as in the first four years of existence (not forgetting the years prior to its opening when individuals kept animals privately for the Zoological Society), there had been very few escapes.

All in fact (apart from the porcupines which presented the very prickly problem recounted earlier) would be better described as mere escapades in which the animals concerned led their keepers a merry dance about the environs of Hazlehead. One suspects they did it for the fun of it, rather than from any serious desire to make a bid for freedom.

Take the case of Foxie who one afternoon decided to go for a stroll, or rather a race, round the park. That day he was being looked after by two members of the Junior Zoo Club, one of whom was holding Foxie, the other his lead.

Due to a misunderstanding, the child who had Foxie in his arms put him down, while at exactly the same moment his comrade dropped the lead. Foxie was off. Round and round the Zoo, then out of the front gates. Seeing what had happened Dennis, the Head Keeper, blew a warning blast on his whistle before setting off in pursuit accompanied by John, another keeper, and a substantial number of the

Junior Zoo Club. The sweat was pouring off the pursuers' faces as they huffed and puffed up and down, chasing Foxie over the lawns, up the paths, round the trees, through the heather garden, until finally, completely breathless, they were forced to sit down and recover.

Seeing his would-be captors tire, Foxie obligingly stopped as well, waiting until they got their second wind. Eyeing them from a distance, his look seemed to be flashing the impatient message: *'Come on! What are you waiting for?'* As soon as the keepers plus children rose to the challenge, Foxie streaked off ahead of them again, prolonging the glorious game of tag, which stopped and started during the whole of the afternoon. Foxie, feeling perhaps that he'd had enough attention paid to him for one day, capitulated at the lily pond by the restaurant where he stopped to quench his thirst. Surrounded by his pursuers, now joined by myself, Foxie rolled over onto his back and allowed me to tickle his white underfur; then quietly acquiesced to having his lead picked up and being led back down to his pen in time for a chicken supper. Nice timing.

The same sort of pattern followed when Taffy, the Zoo's male dingo, broke loose with a spectacular nocturnal leap over the very high fence of his enclosure. A fence which, incidentally, I had been assured would be ample to keep in the most energetic dingo. His escape was not discovered until 7.00 the next morning when I was on my first round of the day. At 8.30 am when the keepers came in, a search party was organised which made its way up to the golf course where a young man with a shotgun was standing.

'Have you seen a dingo?' the search party asked.

'No' came the reply from the shotgun owner. *'I'm looking for the fox that's mauled some of my sheep'.*

'Well, be sure you don't shoot our dingo by mistake', retorted the search party, turning back to hunt for Taffy.

It proved fruitless. Ten o'clock saw the search party come back empty handed. Taffy was still missing. Later in the day however, fresh hope came with a phone call from the local Riding School. Taffy had been spotted. Could someone come from the Zoo and collect him? At the same time, the phone call threw some interesting light on the reason for Taffy breaking loose. There was a bitch at the Riding School in heat.

The search party went out again and sure enough, near the Riding School, they saw Taffy. Irene, the girl who was in charge of the dingoes, shouted his name. He pricked up his ears, bounded towards her and, his amorous adventures presumably over, lay in her arms, while she staggered the quarter of a mile back to the Zoo under his 70 odd pounds. But the matter wasn't finished yet. That evening the Zoo had a visit from the police. One farmer, angry at the loss of his sheep had put two and two together and had decided that Taffy was the sheep marauder. I duly showed the police (who wanted to see if Taffy had any tell-tale marks of blood upon him) to the shed where the dingo had been put until the height of the fence could be raised. They watched at the door as I lifted Taffy's paws up for inspection. '*No blood*' I said. They believed me. If a wild dog was as tame as to let its keeper handle it, it wasn't the kind of animal to wantonly attack sheep. Still they preferred not to enter the shed themselves to inspect Taffy. Tame as he might be, they were not taking any chances.

Another escape that was 'just for fun' was that of Rolf, the Zoo's male Bennett's Wallaby. Rolf and his two females, Margaret and Wendy, had come to the Zoo shortly after it opened. Not from Australia, as you might expect, but from the Kingdom of Fife where they'd been bred by sheep farmer Tom Spence, who also kept some 40 acres of private zoo. This included emus, cheetahs, gibbons, a parrot house, as well as a breeding colony of 30 wallabies.

It was agreed that a few Bennett's wallabies would fit ideally into the scheme of things at Aberdeen Zoo. Their small grey and brown furry bodies, pointed alert faces and Bambi-type air of defenceless innocence guaranteed that they would be a sure-fire attraction with visitors. Equally, in size and in the gentleness of their temperament, they were perfectly suited to the special nature of the Zoo. Therefore, when two ladies of the Senior Zoo Club presented us with a cheque for £160 which they had raised through making Swiss milk tablet, we jumped at the chance of purchasing some wallabies. We did some quick mental arithmetic and found we could afford three.

As had been expected Rolf, Margaret and Wendy settled easily into their new home, a grass area some 20 by 10 feet between the seal pool and the sun room. Accustomed to the inclemency of the Scottish weather they lived out of doors, only using their triangular shelters for an occasional snatch of privacy. Their appetites were good, always a sure sign that animals are settled. They ate their flaked maize, raw vegetables, bread and apples – and showed a great liking for peanuts! Margaret swelled with a joey. We were delighted. Everything, you might say in the enclosure was lovely. Until the day Rolf decided to play ball in a soccer game.

It was a Saturday afternoon in December with a nip in the air, and underfoot the puddles were crunchy with half-thawed ice. Overall, there was a dank mistiness that gave Hazlehead Park an ethereal quality, the trees standing out like spectral sentinels. Outside the Zoo a few children were playing, further off on one of the rugby pitches a group of hardy rugby players were limbering up. Inside the Zoo, it was practically deserted, the few visitors keeping on the whole to the warmth of the indoor exhibits. Nearby, I was disconsolately inspecting the wallaby enclosure. The melting frost had soaked all the ground turning the green grass in to a muddy morass. In the hollows there were puddles like mountain lochs.

There had been nothing but trouble with drainage since the Zoo opened; flat land, rock and a thin top soil with nowhere for the water to run. Nothing to do but introduce artificial drainage. *'We'll have to start putting the drains in next week,'* I said turning to Dennis, *'We'll move the wallabies out of the way down to the little enclosure by the main gate. Might as well get it done now'.* Unfortunately, wallabies are highly nervous animals. Try to get near one and it will shoot off like a bullet from a gun – quivering from its head to the tip of its long tail. If you confine a wallaby in a small space and try and catch it, the animal will panic. It starts, literally, to sweat with fear, from glands under the jaw and the wrists. You can easily kill a wallaby simply by working it up to a state of extreme terror.

But Rolf, Margaret and Wendy were accustomed to us and so remained quite unperturbed when the two keepers entered their enclosures. Dennis quickly grabbed Wendy by the tail in the time-honoured method of moving wallabies. Using it as a rudder, he gently steered his hopping captive out of the enclosure. The other two followed obediently behind while I brought up the rear of the procession. Operation Wallaby went well at first. Dennis manoeuvred Wendy down the path, past the free flight aviary, the donkey paddock and the goats to the main gate and into the temporary enclosure. With Wendy safely inside he turned to direct Margaret in, while Rolf sat placidly, his ears swivelling around a full ninety degrees, constantly at the ready for strange sounds.

It's an old saying that troubles never come singly, which in this case is certainly true. A little girl who'd just entered the Zoo saw Rolf sitting there. She rushed forward shouting excitedly, obviously intent on stroking the appealing little animal. Rolf started bounding away from her towards the main gate. A sudden gust of wind blew the gate open. Rolf shot out.

One unhappy child and two stunned keepers watched the tail end of a wallaby bounding through the wintery park. *'Get the catching net,'* I shouted to Dennis before chasing off in hot pursuit. If you've ever tried to chase the wind, you'll have some idea of what we were up against. Like an arrow from a bow, Rolf shot off into the

Maple back behind bars

SIX months to the day since the Aberdeen Zoo's male porcupine decided to try his luck in the wide open spaces, he was back in his enclosure at the zoo.

It was in August that Maple escaped for the second time from the zoo. On the first occasion he was recaptured by Dr Lil de Kock at Bieldside after only a few days' freedom.

Maple, one of a pair of porcupines, was gifted to the zoo on June 1 last year by Calgary Zoo. His mate, who it is believed was freed by an intruder, is still at large somewhere in the area.

Kestrel back

THE KESTREL stolen from Aberdeen Zoo on Sunday night was back in his cage last night tucking into a hearty meal.

And it was thanks to the coverage of the theft in yesterday's issue of "The Press and Journal" that the kestrel was retrieved by police, said zoo manager Mr George Leslie.

Police returned the bird to him unharmed yesterday and said they would give him a fuller report next week.

There is still no sign of the crane's egg stolen late on Tuesday night.

Is Taffy the dingo a sheep killer?

Sunday Express Reporter

TAFFY THE dingo had the wanderlust, and now he is in disgrace since he broke out of Aberdeen Zoo for a night of freedom.

Zoo manager George Leslie has just received a letter from a local farmer claiming payment for seven sheep which he claims had to be killed after being mauled by Taffy.

Mr. Leslie said: "When we discovered Taffy was missing we organised a search party, but it wasn't until the next day that we found him.

"But, quite frankly, I don't believe he mauled the sheep. A dingo is a coward and if it is going to kill it will make sure of the job."

Convinced

The sheep belonged to farmer James Middleton, of Smithfield Farm, which is near the zoo. He is convinced the dingo was responsible.

However, Mr. Leslie points out: "While we were out looking for the dingo we met Mr. Middleton's son. He was out with his shotgun and said he was looking for a fox.

"To my way of thinking, it's more likely that the fox mauled the sheep."

Now Taffy, who came to Aberdeen from the Welsh Mountain Zoo, has been securely locked up until his fence can be made escape-proof.

Parrot missing from Aberdeen Zoo

A PARROT which was broken nocturna was noticed indigenously disappeared and seeming to appeared to have could up upon a man's Short have flown and became the next disappeared from Aberdeen Zoo's said after recent to was a him being driven on. I've was The was the last parrot age 50 family. Leslie such taske Lila a prid on Tuesday a peak and possibly.

Macaws back in cage

The two macaws which escaped from the aviary at Duthie Park on Sunday have both been recaptured. A park official said that when he went away home the macaws that morning both had gone.

The first macaw was recaptured a few hours after it escaped and the second was retrieved during the night.

distance - down the path, out of the park's main gate, over the road, across the car park and into the fields beyond. A good way off I followed determinedly. Meanwhile over on the rugby pitch 18 rugby players, whose match had been cancelled, were playing nine-a-side football. They were astonished to see a little grey kangaroo bound onto the pitch. They stopped and looked at Rolf. Rolf stopped and looked at them. *'Do you want it caught?'* shouted one of the players – rather unnecessarily under the circumstances – to the approaching figure of myself. *'You can try'*, I roared back between gasps, *'but I doubt if you'll manage'*.

Rolf certainly knew a game when he saw one. He stood watching the men encircle him, his ears twitching, then at the last possible moment he nipped out from under their legs. For a little wallaby he seemed to know all the tricks of the rugby game. Hopping along in a straight line, swerving just at the right minute to avoid being tackled, Rolf would have made an excellent addition to any team. Up and down the pitch the 18 men, now joined by myself, ran trying to catch Rolf who bounded this way and that. Until, tiring of the game, he shot off the pitch and onto the first tee of the golf course. The rugby players followed. Rolf hopped onto the 18th tee and into a small thicket of trees. This proved to be his undoing. Seeing him hampered by the bushes and low branches, the team redoubled their efforts. They fanned out round the thicket and closed in. The game of hide and seek was drawing to an end. One spectacular rugby tackle later and Rolf was taken.

For all Rolf's timidity, we said later that the wallaby seemed to have enjoyed his escapade. All the time the players had been closing in on Rolf, we had kept a careful eye out for any tell-tale patches of sweat on Rolf's jaw and wrist that could have indicated that the animal was in a state of terror. Had those appeared we would have called the game off. But Rolf hadn't started to sweat, nor did he do so when he was captured. He gave no resistance when he was handed over. It seems that from his point of view it had all been good fun.

Knotting Rolf into my anorak, I carried him back to the Zoo, reflecting as we went how fortunate that it was Rolf who had escaped and not Margaret who was carrying young. Had Margaret escaped and panicked, the jolting would probably have thrown the joey from her pouch and killed it.

Back at the Zoo, we released Rolf into his enclosure. Dennis, who had been searching vainly for me to give me the catching net, had given up and returned to the Zoo, where he fed Rolf some bread. Taking it carefully between his delicate paws, he squatted on his hind legs, nibbling away contentedly. Behind him his two wives hopped around completely unperturbed by his comings and goings.

Meanwhile back in our house, another wife wasn't taking the afternoon so stoically. Picking up the muddy, torn anorak that had just done duty as a wallaby catching net, my wife consigned it to the dustbin. She wasn't quite sure if that was the ninth or tenth jacket I had ruined. She'd lost count.

(top – bottom) – Oddjob, the tortoise, giving a ride, grey seals performing for the crowds and school children fascinated by the guanaco

Aberdeen Zoo Facebook Page

It is clear from the Aberdeen Zoo Facebook page that many people have fond memories of the Zoo and I have featured some quotes below.

I remember the wolves howling at night when I went to bed.
Kathy Christie

I worked there for two years before working at Edinburgh for 2 years, Chester for 22 years and another 2 at Edinburgh in 1997. It gave me a good head start in the zoo world.

Used to go there a lot and it was great.
Theresa Rae

I remember feeding a baby lion with a bottle and watching Lulu and Humphrey playing and cuddling. I also recall looking on in wonderment at Victoria and MacNicol with their paws on my uncle's shoulders.
Tracy Radway

Brings back fantastic memories of the Zoo as a kid especially as I got in for nothing being related to George and Margaret.
Rob Stronach

Loved the zoo - I worked there for two years just before it closed.
Leslie Carnie

Us Oakbank school boys did a lot of work in the Zoo. We had a zoo at Oakbank and we gave Aberdeen Zoo all our animals.
George Baxter

Part Four – Conclusion

In my introduction I commented that this book would not have been written without the encouragement of my family and friends who were regaled by the stories of my upbringing at Aberdeen Zoo. I had a conversation with John Buchan, Head Keeper at the time, who was surprised at the number of people in Aberdeen who didn't realise that there was once a zoo in Aberdeen which housed lions, bears, monkeys and chimpanzees. I am therefore pleased that I have eventually utilised all my father's notes and taken the time to chronicle this small part of Aberdeen's history. As my friend Mark said, *'If you don't do it, no one else has the knowledge and you had better do it before you pop your clogs'*.

During the research my grey cells were stimulated into remembering many people and episodes from the past and all this made me question whether I enjoyed the experience. I can tell you I did. I also reflected on where the Zoo Project went wrong and the degradation of the natural world since that time.

Regarding the demise of the Zoo, I hope I have shown a balanced view on the factors which caused its eventual failure. In reality no one person or event was responsible. The change in attitude of Aberdeen City Council was a large factor, but it is perhaps not surprising. I belatedly came across a press cutting in which Dr Lil de Kock mooted the idea to the then Lord Provost Stephen back in the early 1960s. It was reported that he gave his immediate and enthusiastic support for the Zoo Project, but that this was not in line with the majority on Aberdeen City Council. Many were sceptical whether Aberdeen and the North East of Scotland had a large enough population to justify the City spending £30,000 to build a Zoo. It is hard to say, but possibly these dissenting voices found themselves in more prominent positions and were able to influence the future trajectory of the Zoo Project.

It could also be argued that the ratio of office bearers in the Society with an academic background far outweighed those with a business head, and this could have contributed to some decisions being taken without a full analysis of the cost implications. In addition, I cannot say that I have seen any evidence that members of the Society were politically astute and may have been misled in its dealings with the politicians. It is important for me to state at this juncture that I have nothing but respect for all the members of the Society, most of whom are listed in Appendix 2, and who worked tirelessly to make the Zoo a reality and to keep it going. It has to be remembered that they had full-time careers and families to support.

I have already paid tribute to the keepers and staff in the relevant section of the book, however I think it is worth repeating that they all did such a fantastic job during their time at the Zoo. A special mention should go to those who were there to the bitter end, as without their dedication the animals would have undoubtedly suffered.

When the Zoo closed its gates in 1977 Aberdeen City Council reduced the area encompassed by the Zoo and created a Pets Corner. This facility was opened in June 1979 and was free to enter. Some 40 years later it is still there, but no longer free. The Council spent a considerable sum of money in 2019 (£750,000 has been reported in the press) refurbishing the remaining building. The pyramidal roof from the free flight aviary section was removed, and one section of the building was converted into an educational resource. I am sure that this resource will be welcomed and well used, and hopefully will introduce our future generations to the beauty of the natural world.

What is the place of zoos in our society? When I was in my 20s and 30s, and certainly once our two sons were born, we would always visit a zoo or wildlife park if there was one close to our holiday destination. Nowadays I am less inclined to do so. However, it is interesting to note that there are still over 80 zoos and wildlife gardens in the UK, although about 10% have failed in the last 20 years. I still see zoos as playing a vital role in educating the public and preserving species from extinction. There are many which do this very well and are to be congratulated, but I am not so sure about the ones who merely want to entertain.

Don't get me wrong, I enjoy nature and in particular birdwatching. I feel that grabbing a pair of binoculars and going for a walk in the countryside, whether here or on holiday, has enhanced my life greatly. When I was lecturing to students, I used to say that my sanity had been preserved during periods of my life when I was under pressure by my interaction with the natural world. However, my wife and sons may not agree! The natural world is a marvellous resource and we abuse it at our peril. A lot of the people who care about the natural world think that the problems with the degradation of the planet are too big for an individual to solve and yet who would have guessed that a Swedish teenager, Greta Thunberg, would manage to galvanise so many into a search for a more sustainable future.

As I get close to completing this book, we are all coping with the restrictions imposed upon us by the coronavirus pandemic. These restrictions have made many of us more aware of the beauty of nature which can be found close to our homes. this has in many cases resulted in a benefit to both our physical and mental health.

The Earth, its natural resources and its creatures are finite, and I would like my grandchildren and their children to enjoy them as I have. I do not want them to be watching archive footage of one of Sir David Attenborough's excellent series with a narrator telling them that the Great Barrier Reef, the Amazonian Rainforest and the Arctic are no longer in existence thanks to man's over-indulgence and recklessness.

Humphrey entertaining the crowds

Appendix 1 – Official Aberdeen Zoo Guide

ZOO ABERDEEN

Official Guide to Aberdeen Zoo

GENERAL INFORMATION

Opening Times: Daily all year round from 10 a.m. to dusk (winter) or 8.30 p.m. (summer).

Admission Charges: Adults 2/6; Children under 16 1/3; O.A.P.'s 1/3; Members: free entry at all times; Associates: six free entries per year; Junior Members: free entry at all times. Organised parties over 25 in number: Adults 2/-, Children (under 16) 1/-.

Dogs are not allowed in the Garden.

First Aid: Please report to the Zoo Shop.

Lost Parents and Children should meet at the Entrance.

The Zoo Shop, which sells gifts, literature and light refreshments, is open daily during Zoo hours.

Prams and Push Chairs are allowed everywhere but in the buildings.

Lecture Theatre: A programme of lectures and films will be arranged and will be announced. A nominal charge of 6d. is made for all lectures and film shows.

Lost Property should be handed in, or sought, at the Entrance Kiosk.

Don't Hesitate to ask questions of the Keepers. They'll be pleased to help.

This is YOUR Zoo, so please **help to keep it clean.**

DON'T FEED ANIMALS

In this Zoo, all feeding of the animals is strictly prohibited. We must insist on this, because in many Zoos that allow feeding, time and time again animals become sick and sometimes die, due to irregular and unrestricted feeding by visitors. Even good food, harmless in itself, can cause trouble when given in uncontrolled quantities or to the wrong animals. It may also cause jealousy and fighting. For these reasons, we ask your co-operation and understanding of this very necessary regulation.

ALSO

Please do not chase or tease any animal. Anyone found doing so will be asked to leave the grounds immediately.

Aberdeen and North of Scotland Zoological Society

Application for Membership

Name: ....

Address ....

....

School and Age (where applicable) .... (years)
I wish to become a Member/Associate Member/Junior Member of the Aberdeen and North of Scotland Zoological Society.

Signature ....

Date ....

Membership. Members pay an annual subscription of two guineas; Associate members pay an annual subscription of 10/-. (Associates take no part in the election of the Council); Junior members pay an annual subscription of 10/-.

The colour photographs were taken by Mr. J. Mackie and Mr. J. Laskaier of Aberdeen Senior Zoo Club.

DINGO

The Australian wild dog or dingo is of particular interest, as it is one of the few Australian mammals that is not a marsupial. It is generally thought that this dog is related to the Pariah dog of India. We have 3 females, which give birth to young each year. This picture shows one of our litters.

MACAW

The Macaws are the largest of the parrots. They are native to South America and are to be found in dense forests. They have a curved beak, strong enough to crack a Brazil nut. There is a variety of species, Scarlet, Blue, and Gold, etc.

The two seen here were imported to Aberdeen in 1937 and donated to the Zoo prior to opening.

187

COMMON SEAL

This is one of the most abundant of the earless seals. They are to be found in northern waters and the Mediterranean. They are yellowish grey with brownish spots, and grow to a length of 6 feet.

Kept in captivity they become very tame, but they are very difficult to rear.

Seen in the Zoo, from time to time, are casualties from the rocks and beaches, brought in by A.A.P.C.A. inspectors.

ST. KILDA SHEEP

This half wild breed of sheep come from the Island of Soay, off the island of St. Kilda.

Their wool is dark brown. The ewe has small horns, but the ram always has large horns, occasionally having as many as 8.

They thrive and breed well in captivity

THE COMMON BADGER

The common badger is found all over Europe. He is essentially nocturnal. He makes his home, a holt, underground and is scrupulously clean.

In the Zoo, we did have badgers in natural conditions but had to move them to different quarters, as they were never seen by visitors.

Cubs are born in the Spring.

MARMOSETS (Photograph by Aberdeen Journals Ltd.)

'Choco' and 'Sonny' the marmosets pictured here are a breeding pair, that produced twins regularly each year. 'Choco', the female was bartered for a packet of cigarettes in South America, where these animals are to be found. The female looks after the offspring during their first week, thereafter being passed to the male, who tends and carries them around, only passing them to the female at feeding times.

GREY SQUIRREL

The Grey Squirrel was introduced into England during the late 19th century. They have gradually spread north, reaching as far as mid Scotland. They are now classed as vermin, and a special licence is required to allow us to retain them in the Zoo.

They are about 18 inches in length, half of which is tail

AFRICAN TREE CLIMBING GOAT

Little Billy was donated when the Zoo was still in the planning stages, so he actually did come in with the fittings.

He prefers to browse off the leaves of trees, even climbing up suitable shrubs and trees to reach them.

Although he has a magnificent pair of horns, which make him look ferocious, he is really very placid

188

GREAT HORNED OWL

This owl is widespread in both North and South America. It feeds amongst other things on cats, skunks and fowl in the wild.

The two seen in the Zoo come from different parts of America, hence the difference in colour. The larger bird is the female. Breeding success is hoped for.

CHIMPANZEE 'HUMPHREY'

Chimpanzees are found in most of equatorial Africa. They are the most intelligent of all the apes. This fact is substantiated by our chimpanzee 'Humphrey', who can, for example, select the right key from a bunch to open a door or paddock. 'Humphrey', from babyhood, was reared by the manager in his home. 'Heather' was wild caught last year, but both are equally intelligent.

CANADIAN TIMBER WOLF

There are quite a variety of wolves to be found in the Northern Hemisphere. In Canada, they are now only found in the more remote parts. The last wild wolf in Scotland was killed in Sutherlandshire during 1743.

The female wolf pictured here was hand reared. All our wolves show placid natures, especially to their keepers, who often play with them.

WEST AFRICAN CROWNED CRANE

The African Crowned Cranes are very elegant birds, with long slender neck and straw coloured crest.

The one shown here is known to be over 30 years old. As a rule they do very well in captivity, only requiring to be kept indoors when there is severe frost, to protect their feet.

DONKEYS

'Ferrie' and 'Elm' are great favourites in the Children's Corner. They are, in fact, mother and daughter, and are two of the first animals donated to the Zoo.

A recent donation has been 'Padraig', a donkey stallion. It is hoped that in due course there will be offspring. Donkeys live to quite a ripe old age.

WILDCAT

The Wildcat is found throughout Britain, and eastwards through central and southern Europe. The British strain can be distinguished by its darker general colour. They are extremely ferocious when cornered. The wildcat pictured here has been in captivity for 6 years. Also to be seen in the enclosure are 2 young ones, which were dug out of a rock den when very young. These allow themselves to be handled.

189

THE FREE FLYING AVIARY

The 'walk through' aviary has been one of the most dramatic and fascinating steps forward in zoo development during recent years. Many excellent examples are to be found in the United States and the Continent. London and Chester Zoos lead the field in this country. Our aviary is naturally more modest than these, but one has the advantage in being closer to the birds.

MALAYAN SHORT CLAWED OTTER

Otters belong to the badger and weasel family but are more completely adapted to aquatic life. The Malayan otter is much smaller than the common otter. 'Kisko', pictured here, was kept as a pet for 4½ years by an airforce lieutenant.

'Ovaltine' his mate was brought from Malaya. They have bred on 4 occasions, this time (Spring 1969) twins. (Photograph by Aberdeen Journals Ltd.)

WILD BOAR

The wild boar of Europe is a fierce animal and not to be meddled with in anyway in the wild. They have four long razor sharp tusks curving from the mouth. These can be used to great advantage for defence and for rooting tubers from the ground.

Our pair were donated by a well known pig breeder, and as can be seen in the picture, are hand tame having been reared from piglet stage in the Zoo.

MINIATURE GOATS

Goats are one of the oldest domesticated animals in the world. It is said that all the various breeds are derived from three different species.

'Papillon', in the picture, is a female of the Pygmy variety.

CANADIAN PORCUPINE

The Porcupine is a rodent found in both the Old World and the New World. It is a pig like animal with a defensive armour of quills. Contrary to common belief, the porcupine cannot project their quills, but must make direct contact with their foe before the quills become embedded, later causing festering sores and eventual death.

Porcupines breed quite well in captivity.

ROE DEER

The habitat of Roe deer is wooded glades and sheltered meadows. They are timid deer, very seldom seen, being mostly nocturnal. They have seldom been bred in captivity, but in the wild they give birth, usually to twins, during May.

Our 4 does and 1 buck were all orphaned at birth, therefore were hand-reared, and are quite tame.

Appendix 2 - Committee Members

Listed below are the people who were credited with being on the various Zoo committees at one time and another. I have highlighted the signatories to the Memorandum and Articles of Association, many of whom were also members of the various Zoo Committees at one time or another. I have added comments where I can remember facts about the individuals. To the others I apologise, as I am sure they carried out their duties with commitment and enthusiasm for the Zoo Project.

Name	Title	Junior Zoo Committee	Comment
Angus, M.	Ms	X	Macaulay Institute
Backett	Professor		
Berrow, M.	Dr	X	Macaulay Institute
Blaxter, J.H.S.	Mr		
Burchill, J.	Miss	X	Aberdeen High School
Carnegie, J.	Mr		
Cavanagh	Mr		
Chapman	Mr		
Clark	Mr		
Clarke, E.M.W.	Miss		
Connon, C.	Mr		Campbell Connon was the first Solicitor to represent the Zoo
Connon, F.C.	Mr		Frank Connon was Campbell's brother
Cooney, E.	Miss	X	
Crawford, E.M.			
Cuthbertson, D.P.	Dr		The Rowett Institute
de Kock, L.	Dr		Lil de Kock was the founder of the Zoo Project
de Kock, P.	Dr		Pierre de Kock - Macaulay Institute and husband to Lil
Dunn, E.	Mr		Ted Dunn was an

Name	Title	Junior Zoo Committee	Comment
			entomologist who housed many exotic species in his home in Mastrick
Dunnet, G.M.	Dr		
Eadie, M.			
Ewen	Mrs		
Findlay, J.	Mr		Major Findlay was the owner of Poyntons Pet Shop on George Street Aberdeen
Fraser, W.F.	Dr		
Gauld, D.T.	Dr		
Holburn	Miss		
Hunt, S.			
Jenkins, D.	Dr		
Laing, R.M.	Mr	X	Bob Laing was an enthusiastic member of the Junior Zoo Committee
Leslie, G.	Mr	X	Manager of the Zoo from 1966 to 1977
Levvy, A.	Mrs		
Mathieson, A.M.	Mr		
McCready	Mr		
McKendrick, A.	Mr		Allan McKendrick was the solicitor to the Zoo - I remember he died quite young
McWilliam, E.	Miss		
Merchant, J.	Miss	X	
Mitchell	Mr		
Morrice, H.B.	Mr		Harry Morrice was Treasurer to the Zoo
Munro, H.	Mr		Hamish Munro, founder of the shoe shop which

Name	Title	Junior Zoo Committee	Comment
			still bears his name
Nicol, F.	Mrs	X	Macaulay Institute
Nisbet, J.D.	Dr		
Nisbet, B.	Dr		I remember Brenda Nisbet as one of the enthusiastic group trying to make the Zoo a reality
Parrish, B.	Mr		Basil Parrish - Torry Marine Research Institute - Convener of the Society after Lil moved to Germany
Phemister, T.C.	Professor		
Phillipson, A.T.	Dr		
Pole	Mr		
Racey, P.	Dr		
Rae	Dr		
Raeburn	Professor		
Ralph, R.	Dr		Bob Ralph - University of Aberdeen - I remember Bob as he was an enthusiastic Secretary to the Society
Robertson, I.	Mr		
Ross	Mr		
Salzen, E.A.	Professor		The last Convener of the Society
Scorgie, J.	Mr		James Scorgie - owner of Scorgie's Grain Merchant and Pet Store on Rose Street, Aberdeen
Scott, P.	Hon. President		Peter Scott, world renowned naturalist and founder of the Wildfowl Trust at Slimbridge
Shanks, P.L.	Mr		
Spence	Mr		

Name	Title	Junior Zoo Committee	Comment
Stevens	Mr		
Ure, A.M.	Dr	X	Alan Ure - Macaulay Institute
Watt, M.W.			
Webster, J.	Mrs		
Wynne-Edwards, V.C.	Professor		Head of Zoology at the University of Aberdeen
Yule	Mr		
Hon Vice Presidents			
Graham, J.M.	Lord Provost		
* Hogg, N.	Lord Provost		

*   Subsequent Lord Provosts were deemed to be Hon Vice Presidents

Appendix 3 – Photograph & Newspaper Acknowledgement

The images on the pages listed below are used by kind permission of D.C. Thomson & Co Ltd.

Pages 1, 3, 9, 12, 30, 43, 47, 48, 49, 54, 55, 57, 63, 64, 65, 66, 67, 68, 70, 71, 75, 79, 80, 81, 85, 86, 87, 88, 91, 92, 95, 101, 104, 105, 108, 115, 116, 119, 120, 121, 122, 125, 151, 152, 154, 159, 165, 169, 180, 182, 186 and back cover

---

The images on the pages listed below are used by kind permission of Mr Gordon Ferrier.

Pages 49, 97, 103, 117, 118, 119, 126 and 196

The images on the pages listed below are used by kind permission of Mr Witek Mojsiewicz.

Pages 42, 43 and 109

The images on the pages listed below are used by the kind permission of the University of Aberdeen – Special Collections Centre.

Pages 22, 23, 24, 25,26, 27 and 28

The image on the page listed below is used by kind permission of Scotsman Publications.

Page 8

The image on the page listed below is used by kind permission of Donald Gray.

Page 50

All other images used throughout the book are derived from the Leslie Private Collection.